Contents

A Collection Of Papers
On Drug Issues In Ireland

2001

Citation:

Moran, R., Dillon, L., O'Brien, M., Mayock, P. & Farrell, E. with Pike, B. (2001).
A Collection of Papers on Drug Issues in Ireland. Dublin: The Health Research Board.

Published by:
The Health Research Board
An Bord Taighde Sláinte
73 Lower Baggot Street
Dublin 2
Ireland
Tel: 00-353-(0)1-6761176
Fax: 00-353-(0)1-6611856
Email: dmrd@hrb.ie
Web: www.hrb.ie

ISBN: 1-903669-02-2

List of Tables

List of Abbreviations

DMRD	Drug Misuse Research Division
DoTSR	Department of Tourism, Sport and Recreation
EDDRA	European Database on Demand Reduction Activities
EHB	Eastern Health Board
EMCDDA	European Monitoring Centre for Drugs and Drug Addiction
ERHA	Eastern Regional Health Authority
ESPAD	European Schools Project on Alcohol and Drugs
EU	European Union
GUM	Genito-urinary medicine
HAART	Highly Active Anti-Retroviral Treatment
HBV	Hepatitis B virus
HCV	Hepatitis C virus
HIPE	Hospital In-Patient Enquiry Scheme
HIV	Human Immunodeficiency virus
HRB	Health Research Board
ICD	International Classification of Diseases
IDG	Inter-Departmental Group on Drugs
IDU	Injecting/Intravenous drug use or drug user
ISP	Integrated Services Process
KPI	Key Performance Indicator
LDTF	Local Drugs Task Force
MHB	Midland Health Board
MWHB	Mid Western Health Board
NACD	National Advisory Committee on Drugs
NAPS	National Anti-Poverty Strategy
NDP	National Development Plan
NDST	National Drugs Strategy Team
NDTRS	National Drug Treatment Reporting System
NEHB	North Eastern Health Board
NPIRS	National Psychiatric In-Patient Reporting System
NUI	National University of Ireland
NWHB	North Western Health Board
PPF	Programme for Prosperity and Fairness

RDTF	Regional Drugs Task Force
REITOX	European Information Network on Drugs and Drug Addiction
SEHB	South Eastern Health Board
SHB	Southern Health Board
UNDCP	United Nations Drug Control Programme
YPFSF	Young People's Facilities and Services Fund
VEC	Vocational Education Committee
WHB	Western Health Board

Acknowledgements

The authors would like to thank very sincerely those people working in the drugs area who gave generously of their time to provide information regarding recent developments in their areas of work. It is not possible to name all these people but the agencies with which they are affiliated are acknowledged as follows:

> Department of Tourism, Sport and Recreation
> Department of Health and Children
> Department of Justice, Equality and Law Reform
> Department of Social, Community and Family Affairs
> Department of Education and Science
> Health Boards, Drug Treatment Facilities and Youth Workers
> Local Drug Task Forces

Thanks also to the voluntary and community groups and academic researchers in universities and research institutes who provided inputs.

The authors would like to thank all those who provided comments on the report, in particular the internal and external reviewers, personnel from Department of Tourism, Sport and Recreation; Department of Health and Children; Department of Justice, Equality and Law Reform and our colleagues at the Drug Misuse Research Division, Tracy Kelleher, Paul Cahill and Brian Galvin.

Particular thanks to Brigid Pike who contributed substantially to Chapter 1, and edited the entire document, and also to Mary Dunne who provided administrative assistance throughout.

Rosalyn Moran
Lucy Dillon
Mary O'Brien
Paula Mayock
Eimear Farrell
July 2001

Introduction

This collection of papers was developed as part of the work undertaken by the Drug Misuse Research Division (DMRD) in the context of its work as Focal Point to the European Monitoring Centre for Drugs and Drug Addiction (EMCDDA).

The EMCDDA is a European Union (EU) institution providing information concerning drugs and drug addiction and their consequences. The EMCDDA works to improve the comparability of drug-related data in the member states, and to disseminate information and co-operate with international bodies dealing with drug-related issues. In fulfilling its role, the EMCDDA co-operates with a network of 'focal points' or national centres dealing with drug-related issues in the member states. This network is called the REITOX network (European Information Network on Drugs and Drug Addiction). The DMRD of the Health Research Board (HRB) is the designated Irish Focal Point for the REITOX network. Focal Points act as an information resource to the EMCDDA in relation to the national situation in each member state and disseminate European-level information nationally.

Each Focal Point, under contract with the EMCDDA, prepares an annual report on the state of the drug problem. The EMCDDA provide guidelines for the content and structure of such documents. The EMCDDA uses information from these reports from the member states when compiling its annual report on the state of the drugs problem in Europe (EMCDDA, 1996, 1997,1998,1999,2000). The Europe-wide reports are available on the EMCDDA and the linked HRB websites as follows - www.emcdda.org and www.hrb.ie. The HRB edits and publishes the contributory Irish national report every three years (O'Brien & Moran, 1998). The annual report for Ireland 2000 is published elsewhere (Moran, O'Brien, Dillon & Farrell, with Mayock, 2001).

The EMCDDA guidelines for the 1999 and 2000 annual national reports included coverage of some 'key issues or topics', which were agreed, by the countries of the EU and the EMCDDA, to be of particular interest. A selection of these key issues form the chapters presented in this document.

Chapter 1 overviews the main institutional mechanisms involved in the implementation of Irish Government strategy in relation to illegal drugs. Thus, the Cabinet Committee on Social Inclusion, the National Drugs Strategy Team, the National Advisory Committee on Drugs (NACD), the Local Drugs Task Forces (LDTFs) and the Young People's Facilities and Services Fund (YPFSF) are described in the context of Ireland's National Drugs Strategy 2001-2008 (2001). This chapter has been updated to take into account the main developments emerging from the publication of Ireland's National Drugs Strategy 2001-2008 (2001).

Chapter 2 provides an overview of the current situation in Ireland in relation to drug-related infectious diseases (HIV, hepatitis B and hepatitis C infection). The chapter shows that such infectious diseases are of concern in relation to Irish injecting drug-users. Risk behaviours such as the sharing of injection equipment and unsafe sexual practices are discussed. The authors point to the need for more research on the societal and familial consequences of drug-related infectious diseases, which have received little attention in the Irish context to date.

Chapter 3 presents findings from a small (n=10) exploratory study of cocaine users. The study is important as there is considerable anecdotal evidence that cocaine use is becoming more widespread in Ireland, as in other European countries, yet there is little research in the area. The increase is occurring in the context of changing socialising patterns, among young people in particular. In addition, drug-service-providers have had little training in the treatment of problematic cocaine use. The ten users interviewed expected to find themselves in social settings where cocaine was available. They tended to use cocaine in some chosen social settings and not in others, and most often its use was combined with the use of alcohol. The need to monitor trends in cocaine use on an ongoing basis is noted. The chapter includes a review of Irish literature and official information sources on cocaine use, e.g. the National Drug Treatment Reporting System (NDTRS), drug seizures/arrests and surveys.

Chapter 4, prepared for the 1999 national report (Moran, O'Brien, Farrell & Dillon, 1999), reviews the Irish literature on women, children and drug use. Although not updated for the present publication, this is an important contribution to the drugs literature, as the information available in Ireland is dispersed (in the medical, social, psychological and grey literature) and has not previously been brought together. The review covers, inter alia, the epidemiology of female drug use; HIV/AIDS and women, children and drug use; drug use among female prisoners; children and drug use; demand reduction; and barriers for women in accessing services.

The term 'drug misuse' as used in this report refers to the taking of a legal and/or illegal drug that harms the physical, mental or social well being of the individual, the group or society.

Rosalyn Moran

References

Department of Tourism, Sport and Recreation (2001). *Building on Experience: National Drugs Strategy 2001 - 2008.* (Final Report of National Drugs Strategy Review Group). Dublin: The Stationery Office.

EMCDDA (1996). *Annual Report on the State of the Drugs Problem in the European Union 1995.* Luxembourg: Office for Official Publications of the European Communities.

EMCDDA (1997). *Annual Report on the State of the Drugs Problem in the European Union 1997.* Luxembourg: Office for Official Publications of the European Communities.

EMCDDA (1998). *Annual Report on the State of the Drugs Problem in the European Union 1998.* Luxembourg: Office for Official Publications of the European Communities.

EMCDDA (1999). *Annual Report on the State of the Drugs Problem in the European Union 1999.* Luxembourg: Office for Official Publications of the European Communities.

EMCDDA (2000). *Annual Report on the State of the Drugs Problem in the European Union 2000.* Luxembourg: Office for Official Publications of the European Communities.

Ireland's National Drugs Strategy 2001 - 2008. (2001). Dublin: The Stationery Office.

Moran, R., O'Brien, M., Dillon, L. & Farrell, E., with Mayock, P. (2001). *Overview of Drug Issues in Ireland 2000: A Resource Document.* Dublin: The Health Research Board.

Moran, R., O'Brien, M., Farrell, E. & Dillon, L. (1999). 'National Report on Drug Issues, Ireland 1999.' Internal document. Dublin: Drug Misuse Research Division, The Health Research Board.

O'Brien, M. & Moran, R. (1998). *Overview of Drug Issues in Ireland, 1997.* Dublin: The Health Research Board.

Chapter 1

National Drugs Strategy and Structural Mechanisms[1]

Rosalyn Moran and Brigid Pike

1.1 Introduction

In April 2001 the Irish Government approved the National Drugs Strategy for 2001-2008 (2001). The National Drugs Strategy Review Group, which was responsible for developing this new Strategy, had begun its task by undertaking an exhaustive review and consultation process. As a result of this process, the Review Group concluded that the approach to the drugs issue taken to date by the Irish Government provided a solid foundation from which all those trying to tackle the drugs problem should work in the future. The Review Group endorsed the existing approach and, in developing the new Strategy, expanded and strengthened the pillars and principles underpinning this approach (Department of Tourism, Sport and Recreation, 2001).

In this chapter the strategic framework and main structural mechanisms for co-ordinating and implementing the strategy are described under the following headings:

1.2 National Drugs Strategy 1996-2000
1.3 National Drugs Strategy 2001-2008
1.4 National Development Plan 2000-2006
1.5 National Co-Ordination and Implementation
1.6 Regional/Local Co-ordination and Implementation
1.7 Evaluation of National Strategies

---

[1] Particular thanks to Ms Kathleen Stack of the Department of Tourism, Sport and Recreation and Ms Mary Jackson of the Department of Health and Children, who provided much background information and informed commentary. The authors acknowledge their co-operation and enthusiasm.

1.2   National Drugs Strategy 1996 - 2000

Since 1996 the Irish Government's drugs strategy has been underpinned by the findings, recommendations and policies established by the two reports of the Ministerial Task Force on Measures to Reduce the Demand for Drugs (1996, 1997). The overall aim of the Irish Government's drugs strategy has been to provide an effective, integrated response to the problems posed by drug misuse and to work in partnership with the communities most affected by the drugs problem in tackling the issues raised.

Arising from this overall aim, the key objectives of Government policy have been to:

- reduce the number of people turning to drugs in the first instance through comprehensive education and prevention programmes;
- provide appropriate treatment and aftercare for those who are dependent on drugs;
- have appropriate mechanisms at national and local level aimed at reducing the supply of illicit drugs; and
- ensure that an appropriate level of accurate and timely information is available to inform the response to the problem.

In line with these overall aims and objectives, four basic principles have underpinned the Government's strategy:

- it is recognised that an effective strategy must encompass a range of responses, which not only address the consequences of drug misuse, but also attack its causes;
- the response to the drug problem must take account of the different levels of drug misuse, which are being experienced around the country. While illicit drug use is a nation-wide phenomenon (particularly the use of drugs such as cannabis and ecstasy), heroin abuse, in view of its public health implications and close association with crime, is currently seen as the most pressing aspect of the problem. A more targeted response is required, therefore, in the areas experiencing the highest levels of heroin abuse;
- the need for all agencies, which have a role in responding to the drug problem, to work together so as to ensure that their individual

contributions form part of an overall coherent and integrated approach; and

- the need to tap the depth of experience and knowledge which community groups and voluntary organisations can bring to a response to the drug problem. It is recognised that there is considerable knowledge and experience among communities in the areas experiencing the highest levels of use. These communities, therefore, must have an opportunity to participate in the design and delivery of the response to the problem in their areas (Flood, 1999).

In line with the above strategy and policy directions, national policies and strategies have undergone considerable changes over the past five or so years, involving a more integrated, inter-agency response to the drugs problem, and greater engagement of local communities in policy-making and implementation (e.g. Integrated Services Process, Local Drug Task Forces, and Young People's Facilities and Services Fund). More recently, greater regionalisation in the implementation of initiatives in the drugs area has been taking place within the framework of the new National Development Plan 2000-2006 (NDP, 2000) and related social partnership arrangements, which, inter alia, prioritise social inclusion as an objective of national development.

At the micro level, a major objective of drug policy in Ireland has been to maintain people in, and restore misusers to, a drug-free lifestyle. In practice, it is acknowledged that this is not an option for a number of citizens in the short term. Accordingly, a pragmatic approach is taken and the importance of the minimisation of risk, i.e. harm reduction, is stressed in treatment and in a number of education and rehabilitation programmes. The emphasis on harm reduction has grown with the concern relating to the public health implications of the growth in AIDS/HIV and hepatitis B and C infections.

1.3 National Drugs Strategy 2001-2008

1.3.1 National Drugs Strategy Review - The Process
A comprehensive review of the National Drugs Strategy was initiated by the Department of Tourism, Sport and Recreation in April 2000. A sub-group of the Inter-Departmental Group on Drugs, which includes representatives of the state

agencies and the National Drugs Strategy Team, oversaw the management of the review. It was assisted by independent consultants.

The objective of the review was to identify gaps or deficiencies in the existing strategy, revise strategies and, if necessary, develop new arrangements through which to deliver the strategies. The review was to identify the latest available data on the extent and nature of drug misuse in Ireland as a whole, attempt to identify any emerging trends and pinpoint the areas with the greatest levels of drug misuse. To be as comprehensive as possible, the review was also required to look at international trends, developments and best practice models (Department of Tourism, Sport and Recreation, Internal Document).

The review involved extensive consultations through invited submissions (over 190 received), discussions with key players in the state, voluntary and community sectors, and a series of eight public regional consultative fora (attendance by approximately 600 people) held throughout the country during June 2000. Over thirty agencies and organisations were invited to make detailed presentations to further assist in the identification of any gaps or deficiencies in the current strategy. These consultations were underpinned by extensive research of international examples of best practice, and a review of various relevant evaluation reports and other literature.

In early 2001 the Review Team published its findings (Department of Tourism, Sport and Recreation, 2001) and the Government approved the National Drugs Strategy 2001-2008 (2001).

1.3.2 Objectives, Aims and Key Performance Indicators

The overall strategic objective of the National Drugs Strategy 2001-2008 is:

> to significantly reduce the harm caused to individuals and society by the misuse
> of drugs through a concerted focus on supply reduction, prevention, treatment,
> and research (Ireland's National Drugs Strategy, 2001-2008, 2001: 8).

The new Strategy endorses the Irish Government's existing approach to tackling the drugs issue. The four 'pillars' of the new Strategy - supply reduction, prevention, treatment and research - focus on the same four issues as in the Government's previous Drugs Strategy (see Section 1.2 above).

The new National Drugs Strategy, however, seeks to strengthen the strategy and sharpen its focus, by:

- welcoming the Government's positioning of the National Drugs Strategy within the wider Social Inclusion policy and the strong commitment to areas of disadvantage in the NDP 2000 - 2006. The Review Team recognises that the best prospects for communities affected by the drugs problem, in the longer term, rest with a Social Inclusion strategy which delivers much improved living standards to areas of disadvantage throughout the country; and
- requiring all state agencies involved in delivering the National Drugs Strategy to specify annual targets in terms of outputs and desired outcomes for their respective programmes and initiatives.

With these broad considerations in mind, the Strategy has identified seven overall aims:

- to reduce the availability of illicit drugs;
- to promote throughout society a greater awareness, understanding and clarity of the dangers of misuse;
- to enable people with drug misuse problems to access treatment and other supports in order to re-integrate into society;
- to reduce the risk behaviour associated with drug misuse;
- to reduce the harm caused by drug misuse to individuals, families and communities;
- to have valid, timely and comparable data on the extent and nature of drug misuse in Ireland; and
- to strengthen existing partnerships in and with communities and build new partnerships to tackle the problem of drug misuse.

To sharpen the focus, the National Drugs Strategy 2001-2008 (2001) specifies objectives and key performance indicators (KPIs) for each of the four pillars - supply reduction, prevention, treatment and research. These are briefly outlined overleaf.

Supply Reduction

The objectives in relation to supply reduction are:

- to significantly reduce the volume of illicit drugs available in Ireland, to arrest the dynamic of existing markets and to curtail new markets as they are identified; and
- to significantly reduce access to all drugs, particularly those drugs that cause most harm, amongst young people especially in those areas where misuse is most prevalent.

These objectives are underpinned by a quantitative KPI, which seeks to increase the volume of opiates and all other drugs seized in Ireland by 25 per cent by 2004 and by 50 per cent by 2008. To support achievement of this KPI, the National Drugs Strategy Review Team (Department of Tourism, Sport and Recreation, 2001) considered that law enforcement resources should continue to be targeted at disrupting the activities of organised crime groups. It welcomed the progress made in legislating against drug-related crime and developments in the prisons in relation to drug treatment services. Additional KPIs include increasing Garda resources in LDTF areas, and strengthening coastal watch and international co-operation, and enhance drugs policy co-ordination within the Gardaí.

Prevention

The objectives in relation to prevention are:

- to create greater social awareness about the dangers and prevalence of drug misuse; and
- to equip young people and other vulnerable groups with the skills and supports necessary to make informed choices about their health, personal lives and social development.

The first KPI sets a quantitative target of bringing drug misuse by school-goers below the EU average and, as a first step, reducing the level of substance misuse reported to ESPAD[2] by school-goers by 15 per cent by 2003 and by 25 per cent by 2007. Specific initiatives include the development and launch of an ongoing National Awareness Campaign highlighting the dangers of drugs; linking the National Drugs Strategy with the National Alcohol Policy; strengthening the links between the Department of Education and Science and the LDTFs and providing educational supports in LDTF areas.

---

[2] European Schools Survey Project on Alcohol and Other Drugs.

Treatment

The objectives in relation to treatment are:

- to encourage and enable those dependent on drugs to avail of treatment with the aim of reducing dependency and improving overall health and social well being, with the ultimate aim of leading a drug-free lifestyle; and

- to minimise the harm to those who continue to engage in drug-taking activities that put them at risk.

Four out of the seven KPIs relate to the quality of treatment services - immediate access for drug misusers to professional assessment and counselling, followed by appropriate treatment within one month; access for under-18s to treatment, following the development of an appropriate protocol; increasing the number of treatment places to 6,000 by the end of 2001, and to a minimum of 6,500 by the end of 2002; and having a service charter in place for each health board by the end of 2002. The Strategy also specifies that the recommendations of the Steering Group on Prison-Based Treatment Services (Irish Prisons Service, 2000) should be implemented as a priority, and that proposals should be implemented to end heroin use in prison by 2008.

The Strategy also requires that, by the end of 2002, each health board should have in place a range of treatment and rehabilitation options as part of a planned progression for each drug misuser, and that the number of opportunities for training and employment for stabilised drug misusers should be increased by 30 per cent by the end of 2004.

Research

The objectives in relation to research are:

- to have available valid, timely and comparable data on the extent of drug misuse amongst the Irish population and specifically amongst all marginalised groups; and

- to gain a greater understanding of the factors which contribute to Irish people, particularly young people, misusing drugs.

The KPIs set targets for the elimination of all major research gaps in drug research by 2003, and the publication of an annual report on the nature and extent of the drug problem in Ireland, which will include a progress report on achievement of the objectives set out in the National Drugs Strategy.

Co-Ordination and Evaluation

Although not designated one of the 'pillars' of the National Drugs Strategy, KPIs relating to the establishment of an efficient and effective framework for implementing and evaluating the Strategy are identified. They include establishing an effective regional framework to support the measures; completing an independent evaluation of the effectiveness of the overall framework; requiring each agency to prepare a critical implementation path for each of the actions listed in the Strategy that are relevant to their remit; and reviewing the membership, workload and supports required by the National Drugs Strategy Team to carry out its terms of reference.

1.4 National Development Plan 2000-2006

The National Drugs Strategy Review Team (Department of Tourism, Sport and Recreation, 2001) welcomed the Government's positioning its approach to the drugs issue within the context of its Social Inclusion strategy, a plank of its National Development Plan (NDP, 2000) for 2000-2006. Social Inclusion became a major aspect of the NDP arising out of agreements between the Government and the social partners, including the NAPS (National Anti-Poverty Strategy, 1998/99; 1999/2000) and the PPF (Programme for Prosperity and Fairness, 2000).

Under the NDP, spending earmarked for social inclusion amounts to Ir£19,077.7 million / € 24,223.7 million. The NDP involves greater devolution to the regional and local levels, with the Border-Midland-West (BMW) and South-East (SE) regions receiving allocations of Ir£112 million / €142.2 million and Ir£10 million / €12.7 million respectively, specifically to combat drug misuse.

The Government's Social Inclusion strategy involves a range of responses that address the causes and consequences of drug misuse. The Government's response can be characterised as supporting general initiatives to tackle social exclusion, and specific initiatives within the Social Inclusion framework but more specifically targeted at drug-related problems. The general initiatives are targeted at issues seen as contributing to the drugs problem, e.g. unemployment, social deprivation (Drug Misuse Research Division, 1999). Such programmes provide scope for agencies and communities affected by the drugs problem, to avail of financial and other resources to tackle the broader problems associated with drug misuse in their communities.

The Government's specific response to tackling the drugs problem is focused around two major initiatives - the Local Drug Task Forces (LDTFs) and the Young People's Facilities and Services Fund (YPFSF). Both initiatives have been largely focused on urban areas, where the drug problem is most acute.

In the following sections the structural mechanisms to plan, co-ordinate, implement and evaluate the National Drugs Strategy 2001-2008 (2001) are described, together with many of the 100 individual actions identified in the Strategy to address specific gaps in the existing drugs strategy, to strengthen each of the four pillars which underpin it, and to ensure the objectives are met.

1.5 National Co-Ordination and Implementation

The National Drugs Strategy Review Team (Department of Tourism, Sport and Recreation, 2001) endorsed the existing arrangement for co-ordinating and implementing roles at national level, with the addition of an Oireachtas Committee on Drugs (see Table 1.1). The roles and functions, as outlined in the National Drugs Strategy 2001-2008 (2001), are described below under the following headings:

    1.5.1 Central Co-Ordination
    1.5.2 Key Government Departments and Agencies
    1.5.3 Research and Information

1.5.1 Central Co-Ordination

At national level, the policy and co-ordination tasks in relation to the drugs issue overlap with the mechanisms to promote Social Inclusion in general in Ireland. Foremost among these mechanisms is the **Cabinet Committee on Social Inclusion**, which gives political direction to the Government's Social Inclusion policies, including the National Drugs Strategy. Chaired by the Taoiseach, this committee receives input on the drugs issue from the Department of Tourism, Sport and Recreation, the Inter-Departmental Group on Drugs (IDG) and the National Drugs Strategy Team (NDST).

TABLE 1.1
Outline of Structural Mechanisms to Deliver National Drugs Strategy 2001 - 2008

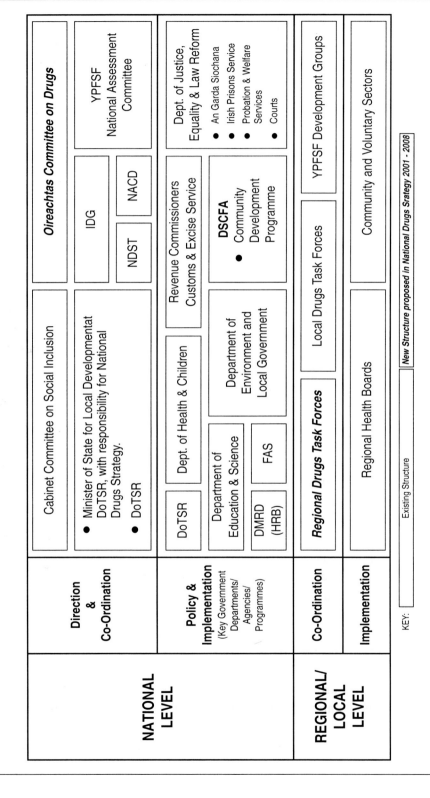

		Oireachtas Committee on Drugs	
NATIONAL LEVEL	**Direction & Co-Ordination**	Cabinet Committee on Social Inclusion	
		Minister of State for Local Development DoTSR, with responsibility for National Drugs Strategy. • DoTSR	IDG NDST NACD	YPFSF National Assessment Committee
	Policy & Implementation (Key Government Departments/ Agencies/ Programmes)	DoTSR	
		Dept. of Health & Children	
		Department of Education & Science DMRD (HRB) FAS	
		Department of Environment and Local Government	Revenue Commissioners Customs & Excise Service
			DSCFA • Community Development Programme	Dept. of Justice, Equality & Law Reform • An Garda Siochana • Irish Prisons Service • Probation & Welfare Services • Courts
REGIONAL/ LOCAL LEVEL	**Co-Ordination**	***Regional Drugs Task Forces***	Local Drugs Task Forces	YPFSF Development Groups
	Implementation	Regional Health Boards	Community and Voluntary Sectors	

KEY: Existing Structure | ***New Structure proposed in National Drugs Srategy 2001 - 2008***

The National Drugs Strategy 2001-2008 (2001) identifies the need for an **Oireachtas Committee on Drugs**. The Strategy includes an action to establish a dedicated drugs sub-committee of the existing Select Committee on Tourism, Sport and Recreation. This Oireachtas committee would meet at least three times a year.

In 1997 the Government appointed a **Minister of State for Local Development at the newly-created Department of Tourism, Sport and Recreation, with special responsibility for Co-ordination of the National Drugs Strategy**. Under the National Drugs Strategy 2001-2008 (2001) the Minister of State chairs the IDG and reports to the Cabinet Committee on Social Inclusion, bringing to its attention any identified issues with a detrimental effect on the implementation of policy. The **Department of Tourism, Sport and Recreation** has responsibility for the overall co-ordination of national policy to tackle drug misuse, including implementation of the National Drugs Strategy 2001-2008. The Department works in partnership with government departments, state agencies and the community and voluntary sectors, through the IDG and NDST. The Department's co-ordinating responsibilities also include the establishment of an evaluation framework for the National Drugs Strategy (see Section 1.7.2 below).

The National Drugs Strategy Review Team (Department of Tourism, Sport and Recreation, 2001) noted that, in other countries, responsibility for co-ordinating drugs strategies usually resides either in the Department of the Prime Minister or the Department of Health. While the advantages of both these options were acknowledged (in terms of political authority, budget size and service-provision experience), the Team recommended retaining the responsibility in Tourism, Sport and Recreation. The Team considered that the Department of Tourism, Sport and Recreation can be objective in relation to all the thematic areas covered by the national policy. Moreover, given this Department's role in local development and co-ordination of a number of different programmes relating to Social Inclusion, and given the correlation between drug misuse and social exclusion, it was considered that it was strategically well placed to take the lead role in co-ordination. In other words, it can bring a holistic and integrated approach to the drugs issue.

The **Inter-Departmental Group on Drugs (IDG)** plays a key role on overseeing the implementation of the National Drugs Strategy. Strengthened under the National Drugs Strategy 2001-2008 (2001) to comprise senior level representatives from government departments, and the chair of the NDST, and to be chaired by the Minister of State at the Department of Tourism, Sport and Recreation, the IDG, inter alia, will advise the Cabinet Committee on Social Inclusion on critical matters of a public policy nature relating to the National Drugs Strategy; ensure timely and effective input by relevant Departments and agencies into emerging operational difficulties or conflicts; and approve the plans and initiatives of the LDTFs and the proposed Regional Drugs Task Forces - RDTFs, and monitor and evaluate the outcomes of their implementation, in conjunction with the NDST. By the end of 2001, the IDG, in conjunction with the NDST, is to develop formal links at local, regional and national levels with the National Alcohol Policy, to ensure complementarities between the different measures being undertaken.

The **National Drugs Strategy Team (NDST)** includes representatives from relevant government departments and agencies, and also two non-government representatives, one each from the community and the voluntary sectors, making the NDTS a partnership between the statutory, community and voluntary sectors. Members of the NDTS play a central role in overseeing the implementation of the Government's National Drugs Strategy by ensuring, inter alia, effective co-ordination between departments, agencies and the community and voluntary sectors, in delivering LDTF and the proposed RDTF plans; reviewing the need for LDTFs in disadvantaged urban areas (particularly having regard to evidence of localised heroin misuse); identifying and considering policy issues and ensuring that policy is informed by the work of and lessons from the LDTFs; overseeing the establishment of the proposed RDTFs; drawing up guidelines for the operation of, and evaluating the action plans of, LDTFs and RDTFs. The NDTS has joint monthly meetings with the IDG, and they jointly report to the Cabinet Committee on Social Inclusion every six months (National Drugs Strategy, 2001).

The **YPFSF National Assessment Committee** was established under the Young People's Facilities and Services Fund (see Section 1.6.3 below), to prepare guidelines for the development of integrated plans in the target areas for the Fund; to assess the plans and to make recommendations on funding to the Cabinet Committee on Social Inclusion. The Committee oversees the implementation of the Fund. Membership of the Committee comprises civil servants, representatives of state agencies and representatives of the community and voluntary sector, and the NDST.

1.5.2 Key Government Departments and Agencies

A number of government departments and agencies play lead roles in developing and implementing policy to tackle the drugs issue in Ireland. Their roles and responsibilities, including new actions assigned under the National Drugs Strategy 2001-2008 (2001), are outlined below. The departments are represented on the IDG, described in Section 1.5.1 above

Department of Tourism, Sport and Recreation

The Department of Tourism, Sport and Recreation has responsibility for the overall co-ordination of national policy to tackle drug misuse, including implementation of the National Drugs Strategy 2001-2008. The Department works in partnership with government departments, state agencies and the community and voluntary sectors, through the IDG and NDST. The Department's co-ordinating responsibilities also include the establishment of an evaluation framework for the National Drugs Strategy (see Section 1.7.2 below). The Department of Tourism, Sport and Recreation also has responsibility for local development, and the implementation of the Integrated Services Process (ISP) *inter alia*. The aims of the ISP include the development of a more focused and better co-ordinated response by the statutory authorities to the needs of communities with the greatest levels of disadvantage. The ISP is aimed at developing an integrated framework within which ongoing programmes can be rationalised and enriched to do a better job of making services available to communities (O'Brien & Moran, 1998).

In early 2001 the Government launched the RAPID (Revitalising Areas by Planning, Investment and Development) Programme, under the aegis of the Department of Tourism, Sport and Recreation. RAPID is a focused initiative by the Government targeting the twenty-five most concentrated areas of disadvantage in the country. The targeted areas will be prioritised for investment and development in relation to health, education, housing, childcare and community facilities including sports facilities, youth development, employment, drug misuse and policing. The programme is based on ISP principles, involving an implementation team (comprising state agency personnel, the local Area Partnership and residents of the local community) and a co-ordinator. Under the National Development Plan, up to Ir£15 billion / €19.5 billion has been earmarked for Social Inclusion measures, and the RAPID programme will prioritise the twenty-five targeted areas and front-load a significant share of this money to them over the next three years.

The Department also has continuing responsibility for providing accessible, positive alternatives to drug misuse through the YPFSF (see Section 1.6.3 below), through arts and culture youth programmes, the schemes run by the Irish Sports Council and the facilities provided under the Sports Capital Programme. The National Drugs Strategy 2001-2008 (2001) states that LDTF areas should be prioritised and specific efforts made to ensure that the groups who are most at risk of drug misuse are actively engaged in recreational activities at local level.

Department of Health and Children

The Department of Health and Children plays key roles in relation to both prevention and treatment of drug misuse. The National Health Promotion Strategy (Department of Health and Children, 2000) outlines a number of objectives relating to drug misuse. The principal aim of the strategy is to support best-practice models for the promotion of the non-use of drugs and the minimisation of the harm caused by drugs. The objectives are to:

- ensure each health board has in place a comprehensive drugs education and prevention strategy;
- continue to support the implementation of existing drug-related health promotion programmes;
- work in partnership with relevant government departments (e.g. Department of Education and Science) and other bodies to co-ordinate health promotion activities; and
- develop prevention and education programmes, with particular emphasis on schools and the youth sector and on interventions in areas where drug misuse is most prevalent.

The National Drugs Strategy 2001-2008 (2001) has assigned the Department the task of launching a National Awareness Campaign highlighting the dangers of drugs, by the end of 2001. The campaign is to promote greater awareness of the causes and consequences of drug misuse not only to individuals but also to their families and to society in general. The Department works closely with the Department of Education and Science in the design, implementation and evaluation of educational programmes. New strategies and actions in this area are discussed below under the entry for the Department of Education and Science.

In relation to drug treatment and rehabilitation, the Department of Health and Children has overall policy responsibility. The Department's policy on the treatment of drug and alcohol misuse stresses the need for community-based interventions including family support and community medical and social services. The Department funds the regional health boards, which provide drug treatment services at regional and local levels (see Section 1.6.5 below). Increasingly, this service provision involves more active liaison with local government structures.

The National Drugs Strategy 2001-2008 (2001) identifies three actions for the Department of Health and Children, designed to maintain the quality of treatment and rehabilitation services - ensuring adequate training is provided for health care and other professionals engaged in the management of drug dependency; consulting all treatment and rehabilitation providers to ensure that performance indicators accurately and consistently reflect the reality of the drug problem locally; and overseeing the implementation of the recommendations of the Benzodiazepine Working Group.

Department of Education and Science

The Department of Education and Science plays a role in relation to prevention, operating mainly through the formal education system. Its initiatives to combat drug use, such as 'Walk Tall' for primary level and 'On My Own Two Feet' for secondary level, and more recently the Social, Personal and Health Education (SPHE) programme, are linked to its overall package of measures to combat educational disadvantage. The National Drugs Strategy 2001-2008 (2001) stipulates that the Department is to ensure that every second-level school is to have an active programme to counter early school-leaving, with particular focus on areas with high levels of drug misuse.

The Department of Education and Science liaises closely with the Department of Health and Children. Both departments are tasked jointly by the National Drugs Strategy 2001-2008 (2001) with providing school-based education and preventive programmes in all schools by September 2003, and ensuring that evaluation is an ongoing element of the 'Walk Tall' and 'On My Own Two Feet' programmes, from 2002 onwards. Moreover, all programmes are to be informed by ongoing research into the factors contributing to drug misuse by particular groups. Parents of at-risk children are to be specifically targeted in school programmes - providing them with access to factual preventative materials, which will encourage them to discuss the issues of coping with drugs and drug misuse with their children. Schools are also to be assisted, through the provision of guidelines, developed by the departments of Education and Health, in co-operation with the health boards, on the formation of a school drug policy.

In the non-formal education sector, the Department of Education and Science works closely with FÁS on joint-funded initiatives such as Youthreach, and in the running of workshops aimed at increasing drug awareness in areas where acute drug problems are apparent. In relation to LDTFs, the role of the Department of Education is to be strengthened under the National Drugs Strategy 2001-2008 (2001). The Department is to publish and implement a policy statement on education supports in LDTFs, including an audit of current supports, by the end of 2001, and to nominate a departmental official to serve on each LDTF.

FÁS

FÁS, the state training agency, operates specific drug-related programmes, including the Special Drugs Community Employment Programme, on which 1,000 places have been assigned for recovering drug misusers. Trained staff are available to work with stabilised drug misusers, to help them access employment or further training. Similarly, advocates, located in severely disadvantaged areas, provide a mentoring service to young people experiencing drug problems.

Acknowledging that the FÁS Community Employment Programme has been an important element of the existing approach to rehabilitation, the National Drugs Strategy 2001-2008 (2001) sets a target for increasing the number of training and employment opportunities for drug misusers by 30 per cent by the end of 2004. The Strategy also identifies the need to examine the potential to involve recovering drug misusers in Social Economy projects, and in other forms of vocational training.

Department of Environment and Local Government

The Department of the Environment and Local Government is responsible for policy and programmes in relation to the environment and for a wide range of services, provided mainly through the local government system. It is also responsible for the local government system, construction industry matters and franchise and electoral systems.

The Department is involved in a broad range of initiatives which are drug-related, e.g. the National Anti-Poverty Strategy (NAPS), and is represented on relevant co-ordination structures. The Department also has a major role in relation to housing, homelessness and estate management.

The National Drugs Strategy 2001-2008 (2001) identifies two actions for the Department, both relating to the issue of homelessness and drug misuse - to commission an external evaluation of the impact of enforcement activity under the Housing Act 1997 on homelessness, and to monitor and evaluate homelessness initiatives in relation to drug issues.

Department of Social, Community and Family Affairs

The Department of Social, Community and Family Affairs' schemes and programmes of support for community development focus on investment in capacity building, so that socially-excluded groups and local communities can be active participants in identifying and meeting their own development needs, working alongside the other social partners.

While the main focus of the Department's programmes is not on drug prevention strategies, rehabilitation etc., local projects working in disadvantaged areas may provide support, in a community development context, to those affected by drug abuse. The Department is represented on the IDG and is to be represented on the proposed Regional Drug Task Forces. Section 1.6.6 below gives an overview of the Dublin Citywide Drugs Crisis Campaign, funded by the Department of Social, Community and Family Affairs, which provides technical assistance and expertise to local communities to develop their capacity to respond to the drugs crisis in their area.

Department of Justice, Equality and Law Reform

The Department of Justice, Equality and Law Reform has overall responsibility for policy and legislation relating to the reduction of the supply of drugs, *inter alia*. In recent years Ireland has put in place one of the strongest legislative frameworks in Europe for countering drugs. Key pieces of legislation include the Criminal Justice Act 1994, the Criminal Justice (Drug Trafficking) Acts 1996 and 1999, the Criminal Assets Bureau Act 1996, and the Proceeds of Crime Act 1996 (Moran, O'Brien, Dillon & Farrell, with Mayock, 2001).

The National Drugs Strategy 2001-2008 (2001) tasks the Department with overseeing the establishment of a framework to monitor the number of successful prosecutions, arrests and the nature of the sentences passed; establishing, after consultation, best-practice guidelines and approaches for community involvement in supply control activities with the law enforcement agencies; reviewing the ongoing effectiveness of crime legislation in tackling drug-related activity; and working with regional health boards in considering how best to integrate child-care facilities in treatment and rehabilitation centres and in residential treatment settings.

The Department also has administrative responsibility for An Garda Síochána, the Irish Prisons Service, the Welfare and Probation Service and the Courts, which, between them, have roles and responsibilities in relation to supply reduction, prevention, treatment and rehabilitation.

An Garda Síochána has responsibility for the State security services and all traffic and criminal law enforcement functions, including those laws related to drug offences. Special units have been integrated into the organisational structure of An Garda Síochána in an effort to address the drugs issue. In each of the country's twenty-seven Garda Divisions, there is a specialised **Drug Unit**, which has responsibility for the enforcement of drugs legislation. There may also be a Drug Unit in a District where drugs present particular problems (Moran *et al.*, 2001).

The **Garda National Drugs Unit (GNDU)** was established in 1995 with specific responsibility for drug law enforcement. The primary focus of the GNDU is to target major drug traffickers, as well as monitoring, controlling and evaluating all drug intelligence and policies within the force. As part of its focus on the national and international aspects of drug trafficking, the GNDU maintains close liaison with police forces from other jurisdictions, through various police networks and operational exchange programmes (An Garda Síochána, 1999). In 1996 the **Criminal Assets Bureau** was set up as an inter-agency response, including An Garda Síochána, the Office of the Revenue Commissioners and the Department of Social, Community and Family Affairs, to target the proceeds of crime, especially drug trafficking. At a community level **Community Policing Fora** have been established on a pilot basis in several LDTF areas. The Garda have also been instrumental in implementing a number of operations addressing supply reduction, including Cleanstreet, Nightcap, Rectify, Tap and Dóchas.

Under the National Drugs Strategy 2001-2008 (2001) it is intended to extend, and enhance the efficiency of, all the above initiatives - adding resources to existing drug units, and establishing drug units in areas where they don't exist; establishing a co-ordinating framework for drugs policy in each Garda District to liaise with the community and act as a source of information for parents and members of the public; increasing the level of Garda resources in LDTF areas, building on the lessons learned from the Community Policing Fora, and extending the Community Policing Forum model to all LDTF areas, if the evaluation of the pilot is positive.

The Gardaí are also active in prevention, particularly in relation to young people involved in, or at risk of becoming involved in, drugs and crime. Initiatives include the Garda Youth Diversion Projects, generally managed by Foróige and/or the City of Dublin Youth Service Board; the Drug Awareness Programme for communities; Garda Schools Programmes; the Garda Mobile Anti-Drugs Unit; and the Juvenile Diversion Project. Garda Juvenile Liaison Officers are also assigned throughout the country. The National Drugs Strategy 2001-2008 (2001) identifies an opportunity for enhanced co-ordination, whereby incidences of early use of alcohol or drugs by young people coming to Garda attention are followed up by the Community Police and/or the health and social services, so that problem-drug misuse may be diagnosed/halted early on.

The National Drugs Strategy Review Team (Department of Tourism, Sport and Recreation, 2001) saw the **Irish Prisons Service** as playing a key role in relation to supply reduction, treatment and rehabilitation. In relation to supply reduction, the threat of imprisonment is seen as both a sanction against and punishment for supply activity. The National Drugs Strategy 2001-2008 (2001) endorses the recommendations of the first report of the Steering Group on Prison-Based Drug Treatment Services (Irish Prisons Service, 2000), and recommends that they be implemented as a priority, together with proposals to end heroin use in prisons by 2008. The Strategy also seeks an expansion of prison-based programmes with the aim of having treatment and rehabilitation services available to those who need them, including programmes dealing specifically with the reintegration of the drug-using offender into the family/community. The Strategy also calls for an independent evaluation of the overall effectiveness of the Prison Strategy by 2004.

The **Probation and Welfare Service** co-ordinates a range of drug treatment initiatives both within the prison setting and post-release, in conjunction with rehabilitation agencies and the community.

Within the **Courts** system, a Drug Court has been established on a pilot basis in north inner-city Dublin. These courts are intended to be treatment oriented, where people with a drug problem, who are charged with non-violent offences, are diverted to treatment programmes rather than prison. The success of the initiative depends on the formulation and implementation of cohesive treatment and rehabilitation programmes, which will help break the cycle of reoffending and ultimately end all criminal activity. If the evaluation of the pilot study is positive, this type of early intervention system is to be introduced in all LDTF areas, accompanied by appropriate familiarisation for the judiciary on the role of the Drug Court (National Drugs Strategy, 2001)

Office of the Revenue Commissioners
The Office of the Revenue Commissioners includes the Customs and Excise Service. Customs have primary responsibility for the prevention, detection, interception and seizure of controlled drugs, intended to be smuggled or imported illegally into the State (Moran *et al.*, 2001).

In 1992 a Customs National Drugs Team was established, with the principal role of directing the work of Customs on the prevention of drugs smuggling and the enforcement of legislative provisions regarding the import and export of controlled drugs and other substances. The Team's units are strategically located around the coast of Ireland in an effort to prevent drug trafficking (Office of the Revenue Commissioners, 1993).

In 1996 a Memorandum of Understanding was agreed between Customs and Excise and An Garda Síochána regarding drugs law enforcement. As a result, a joint task force comprising Customs, Garda and the Naval Service was established, and personnel are exchanged at national level, and liaise at local level. Customs also liaise with the Garda National Drugs Unit and the Criminal Assets Bureau. Customs have also entered into agreements with trade associations and individual companies regarding detection of illegal drug smuggling, and developed a Coastal Watch Programme, which enlists the help of coastal communities and seagoing personnel in reporting suspicious activities. At an international level, the customs services of all EU member states are linked electronically to facilitate quick and effective exchanges of information. A Customs official has been assigned to the Irish Embassy in London, and appointments are to be made to Europol in The Hague.

Under the National Drugs Strategy 2001-2008 (2001), these initiatives are to be strengthened and consolidated. Close liaison and collaboration, both nationally and in conjunction with enforcement and intelligence agencies in Europe, are to be developed; coastal watch and other port-of-entry measures to restrict importation of illicit drugs are to be strengthened; and a Customs official is to be assigned to the Europol National Unit. The Customs and Excise Service is also to develop benchmarks, in conjunction with the Gardaí, against which seizures of heroin and other drugs can be evaluated under the EU Action Plan on Drugs (Commission of the European Communities, 1999), in order to establish progress on a yearly basis.

1.5.3 Research and Information

An Interim Advisory Committee on Drugs was established by the Cabinet Committee on Social Inclusion in recognition of the importance of having authoritative information and research findings available as a guide to policy. The Committee was chaired by the then Minister of State with special responsibility for National Drugs Strategy, Chris Flood, TD, and later Eoin Ryan, TD. The Committee reported in February 2000 and, *inter alia*, made a number of recommendations regarding the structure and composition for a National Advisory Committee on Drugs, and recommendations for a three-year programme of research and evaluation on the extent, nature, causes and effects of drug misuse in Ireland.

National Advisory Committee on Drugs

The National Advisory Committee on Drugs (NACD) was established in July 2000. The Committee was established on a non-statutory basis for three years and has responsibility for research and information on drug misuse in Ireland and for a three-year prioritised work programme of research and evaluation.

The functions of the Committee are as follows:
- to advise the Cabinet Committee on Social Inclusion and through it, the Government, in relation to the prevalence, prevention, treatment and consequences of problem drug use in Ireland, based on the Committee's

analysis and interpretation of research findings and information available to it;

- to review current information sets and research capacity in relation to the prevalence, prevention, treatment and consequences of problem drug use in Ireland and to make recommendations, as appropriate, on how deficits should be addressed, including how to maximise the use of information available from the community and voluntary sectors;
- to oversee the delivery of a three-year prioritised programme of research and evaluation, as recommended by the Interim Advisory Committee, to meet the gaps and priority needs identified by:
    - using the capacity of relevant agencies engaged in information gathering and research, both statutory and non-statutory, to deliver on elements of the programme;
    - liaising with these agencies with a view to maximising the resources allocated to delivering the programme and avoiding duplication;
    - co-ordinating and advising on research projects in the light of the prioritised programme; and
    - commissioning research projects, which cannot be met through existing capacity;
- to commission additional research at the request of the Government into drug issues of relevance to policy;
- to work closely with the Drug Misuse Research Division of the Health Research Board on the establishment of a national information /research database (in relation to the prevalence, prevention, treatment and consequences of problem drug use) which is easily accessible; and
- to advise relevant agencies with a remit to promote greater public awareness of the issues arising in relation to problem drug use and to promote and encourage debate through the dissemination of its research findings.

The first meeting of the Committee took place in late September 2000. It has formulated a three-year work programme under six general headings, as itemised below:

Inventory of Research and Information

- compile a comprehensive inventory of existing research and information sets relating to the prevalence, prevention, treatment/rehabilitation and consequences of problem drug use in Ireland;

Improved Co-ordination of Research and Data Collection

- open communication channels with key agencies to ensure that the NACD is kept informed of any new research being undertaken or new data being collected;
- establish a research network which will ensure better co-ordination and integration of research projects among relevant agencies and maximise resources in the context of the NACD's programme of research;

Prevalence

- determine the size and nature of the drug problem in Ireland;
- determine the extent and nature of opiate use, poly-drug use and patterns of problem drug use (experimental, occasional, regular non-medical use) particularly among young people under 25;
- identify emerging trends and geographical spread;
- determine the extent and nature of problem use of prescription drugs;
- determine the prevalence of problem drug users not in contact with treatment services;

Prevention

- examine the effectiveness in terms of impact and outcomes of existing prevention models and programmes, with particular regard to evaluation instruments developed at European level;
- undertake comparative studies of different models with particular reference to those in operation in Task Force areas;
- determine transferability of models among different target groups;

Treatment/ Rehabilitation

- examine the effectiveness in terms of impact and outcomes of existing treatment and rehabilitation models and programmes;
- undertake longitudinal studies of the effectiveness of existing treatment and rehabilitation models;
- examine the context in which relapse occurs;
- examine the impact of the treatment setting;

Consequences
- examine the cost to society of the drug problem in terms of:
  - drug-related deaths;
  - impact of drugs on the family and communities;
  - relationship between drugs and crime; and
  - methods for tackling social nuisance related to drug misuse.

The National Drugs Strategy 2001-2008 (2001) has specified that the NACD should examine its three-year research programme to establish whether it can:

- carry out studies on drug misuse among at-risk groups;
- commission outcome studies to establish the current impact of methadone treatment on both individual health and on offending behaviour; and
- conduct research into the effectiveness of new mechanisms to minimise the sharing of equipment.

Drug Misuse Research Division
The Drug Misuse Research Division (DMRD) is a division of the Health Research Board (HRB), a statutory body based in Dublin, and is involved in national and international research and information activities in relation to drugs and their misuse. The DMRD is funded by national and EU sources and contract research. International collaborators include the EMCDDA and Council of Europe Pompidou Group.

The DMRD maintains and develops the national epidemiological database on treated drug misuse in Ireland - the National Drug Treatment Recording System (NDTRS). The NDTRS provides comprehensive data on the numbers and characteristics of those treated for drug misuse in Ireland.

Current and recently completed research studies include research into trends in drug misuse; knowledge, attitudes and beliefs regarding drugs and drug users; drug service provision; crèche availability and use in drug treatment contexts; drug use, impaired driving and traffic accidents; drug use by prisoners and drug use in rural areas.

The DMRD is involved in information and dissemination activities at national and European levels. It publishes research studies on an ongoing basis. These publications are made available to all public and relevant specialist libraries in Ireland. The DMRD also publishes DrugNet Ireland twice yearly.

National Documentation Centre

On foot of the report of the Interim Advisory Committee on Drugs, the Drug Misuse Research Division was nominated to establish a National Documentation Centre. The Government designated the Health Research Board as a central point to which all information on drug use in Ireland should be channelled. (Press release : Minister of State, Eoin Ryan establishes NAC on Drugs, July 2000). The National Documentation Centre will include a drop-in access point and library facility focusing on grey literature in the drugs area, development of an electronic library and, in collaboration with the EMCDDA, a virtual library, which will provide access to a pan-European information network on drugs. In the long term it is planned that this resource will be entirely electronically based. Related added-value activities envisaged include regular publication of a Register of Research on Drug Misuse in Ireland and Annotated Bibliographies on Drug Misuse in Ireland. An information and dissemination function will be an integral part of the Documentation Centre.

1.6   Regional/Local Co-Ordination and Implementation

The National Drugs Strategy Review team (Department of Tourism, Sport and recreation, 2001) welcomed the embedding of the Government's approach to the drugs issue within the context of its Social Inclusion strategy. Consequently, it endorsed the existing regional and local structure of roles and responsibilities, which are funded through the NDP. To strengthen co-ordination at regional level, the National Drugs Strategy 2001-2008 (2001) has proposed the establishment of Regional Drug Task Forces (see Table 1.1).

1.6.1 Regional Drug Task Forces

All regional health boards currently have co-ordination structures in place (Regional Drug Co-ordination Committees) and have appointed Drugs Co-ordinators. The National Drugs Strategy 2001-2008 (2001) calls for the establishment of a Regional Drugs Task Force in each health board area (including the three health board areas in the ERHA), incorporating and expanding the work of the Regional Co-Ordination Committees (Department of Tourism, Sport and Recreation, 2001). The NDST will oversee this development. The membership and working arrangements adopted by the LDTFs will apply to the RDTFs.

The National Drugs Strategy 2001-2008 (2001) proposes that the RDTFs will include representation from the local authority, VEC, health board, departments of Education and Science and of Social, Community and Family Affairs, An Garda Síochána, Customs and Excise, Probation and Welfare Services, FÁS, area-based partnership, and the voluntary and community sectors.

The roles of the RDTFs will be, *inter alia*, to ensure the development of a co-ordinated and integrated response to tackling the drugs problem in their region; to create and maintain an up-to-date database on the nature and extent of drug misuse and to provide information on drug-related services and resources; to identify gaps in service provision; to prepare a development plan to respond to regional drugs issues for assessment by the NDST and approval by the IDG; to provide information and regular reports to the NDST and to develop regionally relevant policy proposals, in consultation with the NDST.

1.6.2 Local Drugs Task Forces

The Local Drugs Task Forces (LDTFs) were established in 1997 with a three-fold purpose - to ensure effective co-ordination of drug programmes and services at local level; to involve communities in the development and delivery of locally-based strategies to reduce the demand for drugs; and to focus actions on tackling the problem in the communities where it is at its most severe. It was hoped that the establishment of the LDTFs would also help offset the feelings of marginalisation and abandonment being felt by these communities. The LDTFs provide a strategic locally-based response by the statutory, community and voluntary sectors to the drug problem in the areas worse effected.

Fourteen LDTFs[3] have been established, in areas experiencing the highest levels of drug misuse and, in particular, where heroin misuse is most prevalent. The LDTFs were mandated to prepare and oversee the implementation of action plans, co-ordinating all relevant drug programmes in their areas and addressing

---

[3] The LDTF areas are Ballyfermot, Ballymun, Blanchardstown, the Canal Communities, Clondalkin, Dublin North Inner City, Dublin South Inner City, Dublin 12, Dun Laoghaire/Rathdown, Finglas-Cabra, North Cork City, North East Dublin and Tallaght. Bray has recently been designated a LDTF area.

any gaps in service. Over 200 separate measures, mainly community-based initiatives, were initially funded to complement and add value to existing services and programmes under the themes of education, prevention, treatment, aftercare, rehabilitation and reducing supply (Department of Tourism, Sport and Recreation, 1999).

The LDTFs comprise representatives from statutory bodies such as the health boards, Garda Síochána, local authorities, FÁS (training agency), the vocational education committees, Probation and Welfare Services, departments of Education and Science and Social, Community and Family Affairs (under discussion at the moment) as well as from voluntary and community groups. It is expected that representatives at a senior level from these agencies be nominated to the LDTFs, i.e. people who are in a position to influence policy. In addition, organisations are required to view staff participation in LDTF activities as core duties and to allocate the time necessary for meaningful participation.

The formal composition of the LDTFs allows for broad representation and, in addition, allows for representation of vocational groups/agencies through the sub-committees and working groups of the LDTFs. Drug users can achieve representation through the use of drug-user fora. Some of these latter groups are campaigning for more direct involvement. LDTFs are required to ensure that appropriate procedures are in place to assist them with the regular review of representation (Department of Tourism, Sport and Recreation, 1999:16). At this stage of the development of LDTFs, formal and informal activists are calling for greater networking and sharing of experiences between LDTFs.

When the LDTFs were being established, an independent chairperson was nominated to each LDTF by the Area Partnership in whose area the LDTF operated. The Area Partnerships were set up in thirty-eight disadvantaged areas around the country (including all the LDTF areas) under the Operational Programme for Local Urban and Rural Development 1994-1999, to address the issue of long-term unemployment, particularly in the context of social inclusion. Subsequent chairperson vacancies have been filled through nomination by the Area Partnership, in consultation with the LDTF and the NDST.

A range of supports have been put in place to assist the LDTFs in their work. Each LDTF has a full-time co-ordinator funded by the relevant health board. Each LDTF has been requested to identify its training needs.

Phase 1 of LDTF Operation - January 1997 to October 1998

The LDTFs prepared action plans for their areas and Ir£10 million / €12.7 million were set aside to finance the plans. This money funded over 200 separate projects, mostly community based and designed to complement and add value to the drug programmes and services already being provided or planned by the state agencies. Although projects were initially funded on a one-year basis, they subsequently received interim funding, pending their formal evaluation and a decision in relation to their 'mainstreaming'.

An evaluation of the LDTFs was concluded in October 1998, which focused on the processes and structures associated with the initiative. The evaluation found that the LDTFs had 'achieved a considerable degree of success in the short term since they were established and that their very existence had provided a strong focus for tackling drug issues in the target areas, often reducing the feeling of isolation felt by local communities and preventing a potentially critical situation from developing further' (PA Consulting Group, 1998).

Subsequently, the NDTS undertook a detailed review of the operation of the LDTFs, taking account of the findings and recommendations of the independent evaluator. In July 1999, the Cabinet Committee on Social Inclusion agreed arrangements for the continued operation of the LDTFs, based on the recommendations brought forward by the NDST, on foot of this review.

Phase 2 of LDTF Operation - October 1998 to October 2000

The proposed new arrangements for the LDTFs included the continuation of the LDTFs for at least a further two years, new terms of reference and the addition of elected public representatives and representatives from the departments of Education and Science and Social, Community and Family Affairs (under discussion at moment) to the membership of the LDTFs. They also included the putting in place of an evaluation framework, which would allow the LDTF initiative to be measured in terms of outcomes and impacts (see Section 1.7.3 below).

In July 1999 the Cabinet Committee on Social Inclusion approved the following terms of reference, revised membership of the LDTFs and designation of LDTF areas for the next phase of the scheme:

New Terms of Reference for LDTFs
LDTF are to:

- oversee and monitor the implementation of projects already approved under their existing action plans;
- ensure the evaluation of current projects, with a view to their mainstreaming by the relevant statutory agencies;
- in accordance with agreed guidelines, prepare updated action plans which:
  - update the area profile and take into account changes in the drug problem since preparation of the original plan; and
  - ensure that emerging strategic issues are identified and propose policies (actions) to address such issues;
- oversee the implementation of the local drugs strategy, in consultation with appropriate voluntary and statutory agencies and community/ resident groups;
- ensure appropriate representation by the voluntary and community sectors on the LDTF;
- identify any barriers to the efficient working of the LDTF;
- develop networking arrangements for the exchange of information and experience with other LDTFs and the dissemination of best practice;
- identify the training needs of LDTF members and take the necessary steps to ensure those needs are met through appropriate courses, training programmes etc.;
- take account of and contribute to other initiatives aimed at tackling social disadvantage under the aegis of the Cabinet Committee on Social Inclusion, including the Integrated Services Process, the Young Peoples' Facilities and Services Fund, the Local Development Programme, the Community Development Programme, etc.; and
- provide such information, reports and proposals to the NDST, as may be requested from time to time.

Each LDTF was asked to prepare updated action plans, following specified guidelines that stress the need for a more strategic approach. The updated action plans are to be structured in three parts - review of progress in implementing the existing action plans; development of a revised strategy; and development and prioritisation of specific proposals to give effect to the revised strategy. The guidelines provided were very detailed and further guidance in the form of information sessions was made available to LDTFs, particularly with reference to compiling and disseminating examples of best practice under the various themes to be addressed in the plans.

Membership of the Local Drug Task Force

Membership is to be as follows:

- expanded to include representatives from the Department of Education and Science and Department of Social, Community and Family Affairs, and it is recommended that locally-elected public representatives be given the option of becoming members; and

Designation of Local Drug Task Force Areas

It was recommended that the focus should be on those areas, where the drug problem is most acute. The criteria to be used in determining such areas should include:

- drug-treatment data from the Health Services;
- Garda crime statistics;
- data relating to school attendance/drop out; and
- other relevant data on the levels of social and economic disadvantage in the area.

Using these criteria it was recommended that Bray be added to the list of designated LDTF areas.

In agreeing these arrangements, the Cabinet Committee on Social Inclusion also allocated a further Ir£15 million / €19.05 million to the initiative over the period 2000-2001. This funding was to enable the LDTFs to update their plans, as well as address issues that needed to be tackled on a cross-Task Force basis. As indicated above, the NDTS has issued detailed guidelines to assist the LDTFs in updating their plans.

Under the revised Drugs Strategy in the National Development Plan, the allocations to combat drug abuse specifically through the LDTFs[4] will be Ir£122 million / €155 million over the seven-year period of the Plan. The allocation

---

[4] Department of Tourism, Sport and Recreation vote.

under the Regional Programmes will be Ir£112 million / €142.2 million, for the SE (South-East) Region and Ir£10 million / €12.7 million for the BMW (Border, Midlands and West) Region (Department of Tourism, Sport and Recreation, Internal Document).

Achievements of the LDTFs

The LDTFs are an innovative response to a serious drug problem, which manifested itself most acutely in a number of deprived communities. Amongst the achievements of the initiative has been the active and constructive community response in areas where resources were few, and the establishment of a broad range of initiatives in the areas of treatment, rehabilitation, education, prevention etc., which address local needs.

Mainstreaming of LDTF projects has been instituted in order to ensure the continuity of projects that are meeting their aims and objectives. The NDST has prepared a set of protocols to govern the mainstreaming of such projects. Fundamental to mainstreaming in this context is the transfer of budgetary responsibility from government departments to agencies/project promoters for specific pieces of work. The exchange is to be consolidated as a formal contract/agreement witnessed by the LDTF. Standards acceptable for Exchequer accounting purposes will apply. These protocols will provide a platform on which project promoters and statutory agencies can enter into an arrangement for the continuous operation of projects on a mutually acceptable basis.

One hundred and forty LDTF projects were evaluated April-June 2000, and 122 were subsequently mainstreamed involving a number of government departments. PR Consultancy coordinated a composite report on the evaluation. Mainstreaming will ensure ongoing funding. The process copperfastens the role played by community and voluntary organisations in responding to drug misuse at a local level.

Documentation provided by the Department of Tourism, Sport and Recreation indicates the following as amongst the achievements of the LDTFs:

- Eight hundred stabilised drug users are participating in specially-designed Community Employment projects developed by the LDTFs, in conjunction with FÁS, the national training agency. These projects, supplemented with treatment and counselling, will assist drug users to improve their employment potential (Department of Tourism, Sport and Recreation, Internal Document).

- The LDTFs have contributed to creating greater awareness about the issues around drug misuse. Nearly 350 schools have undergone drug awareness programmes in LDTF areas, with around 6,000 school-children participating in these programmes. In addition, 350 teachers have received training. Over 300 youth groups have run drug-prevention initiatives; training programmes have also been delivered to 1,300 community workers, 1,200 parents and 1,300 young people outside the school setting. These programmes are aimed not only at creating greater awareness of the dangers of drug misuse among young people, but also at educating communities about the needs of drug users, so that they are in a better position to respond to these needs (Department of Tourism, Sport and Recreation. Personal Communication). Evaluation of the LDTFs will be ongoing.

1.6.3 Young People's Facilities and Services Fund

An innovative and interesting feature of policy in the drugs area in Ireland has been a focus on the potential of sport and recreation to engage young people constructively and thereby discourage or divert them from involvement in drugs and unhealthy life choices.

Under an initiative separate from but complementary to the LDTF initiative, the Government set up the Young People's Facilities and Services Fund (YPFSF). The aim was to develop youth facilities, including sport and recreational facilities, and services in disadvantaged areas where a significant drug problem exists or has the potential to develop. The three-year Fund aims to attract young people in those areas, who are at risk of becoming involved in problem drug use, into more healthy and productive pursuits. The target group for this Fund is youth aged 10 to 21 years who traditionally have found themselves outside the scope of mainstream youth activities because of their family background, their involvement in crime or drug misuse or their lack of education.

The primary focus of the YPFSF is the LDTF areas, and the six Urban Areas of Galway, Limerick, South Cork City, Waterford, Bray and Carlow, where serious drug problems exist or have the potential to develop.

Development Groups in the thirteen LDTF areas, and six additional Urban Areas, were established to develop plans and strategies for the YPFSF and to oversee their implementation in conjunction with the relevant VEC and local authority. In the LDTF areas, the Development Groups comprise one representative each from the LDTF, the VEC and the relevant local authority. In the targeted Urban Areas, the local VEC has responsibility for the development and delivery of the strategies, in conjunction with relevant state agencies and the community and voluntary sectors.

To ensure complementarity with the LDTFs plans for the area, the LDTFs nominate a representative, who generally acts as chairperson to the Development Groups. The YPFSF plans and implementation process reports are passed to the LDTFs for their information and views, before submission to the National Assessment Committee (see Section 1.5.1 above), which evaluates them and recommends funding to support their implementation. The Development Groups are responsible for overseeing the effective implementation of the plans.

YPFSF outside the LDTF Areas

Recognising that the issue of problem drug use is not confined to the Urban Areas, YPFSF funding has been allocated to a number of nation-wide initiatives to inform and raise awareness of the dangers of problem drug use, particularly through peer education. Up to Ir£7.2 million / €9.14 million has been allocated under the YPFSF for the Springboard Initiative, which will see the establishment of fourteen family support projects aimed at children at risk in disadvantaged areas around the country.

YPFSF Budget[6]

The YPFSF was established in 1998 with Ir£30 million / € 38.1 million allocated over three years. This has since been increased to Ir£37.4 million[7] / € 47.5 million. Of this amount, Ir£27.4 million / € 34.8 million has been approved for support of over 295 projects in the LDTF areas. The remaining Ir£10 million / €12.7 million (approximately) has been allocated as follows:

---

[6] Acknowledgements to K. Stack of the Department of Tourism, Sport and Recreation, and S. Falvey of the Department of Education and Science, for supplying budgetary information.

[7] This funding is separate to LDTF funding, and is in Department of Education and Science vote.

- Ir£7.2 million / €9.14 million over three years (1998-2000) has been allocated to the Springboard Initiative, which is administered by the Department of Health and Children. Springboard funds fifteen family support projects. The projects work intensively with mainly 7-12 year olds (who are at risk of going into care or getting into trouble) and their families.
- Ir£2.3 million / €2.9 million was allocated to other urban areas outside the LDTF areas for prevention work, e.g. Waterford, Galway, South Cork City, Limerick, Bray and Carlow.
- Ir£0.5 million / €635,000 goes to voluntary organisations who have the capacity to deliver drug prevention programmes at national or regional level. This was a new initiative in 1999.

In terms of the new structures set up under the National Development Plan, the breakdown of this money is as follows:

- South and Eastern Region: Ir£29.756 million / €37.782 million
- Border Midlands and Western Region: Ir£0.450 million / €0.571 million
- Department of Health and Children: Ir£7.200 million / €9.142 million
- Total: Ir£ 37.406 million / €47.496 million

The type of projects and initiatives approved as part of the plans and strategies submitted to date include:

- capital projects such as building, renovating or fitting out **community centres, youth facilities and sports clubs** so as to provide suitable accommodation for programmes and services geared for the most 'at risk' young people in an area. Access for the target group is an essential condition of funding for capital projects;
- a number of **purpose-built youth centres**, which will provide a focal point for youth activities in an area, particularly areas such as Tallaght, Ballymun, Clondalkin and Blanchardstown, where there is a dearth of dedicated youth facilities;
- the appointment of **youth and outreach workers** to work on the ground with the target group, offering developmental activities and educational programmes for young people who have traditionally found themselves outside the scope of mainstream youth work owing to family background, involvement with crime or drug misuse or lack of education;

- the appointment of **sports workers** to encourage greater involvement of the target group in sports and recreational activities;
- a wide variety of **community-based prevention/education programmes**, including Early School Leaving Programmes, Sports and Recreational Activities, Family Support Programmes, Art, Drama and Music Programmes, Counselling and Transport Services;
- **targeted interventions** for particular groups such as youth work projects for young travellers;
- the appointment of **national drugs education and training officers** for youth organisations catering for the target group who will deliver programmes throughout the organisation; and
- a provision to meet the training needs arising from the Fund, particularly in the area of drugs training for youth workers.

Innovative measures, which can serve as a model for such projects, have been applied to the draw-down of funds under the YPFSF. These measures ensure that the most deprived groups will have access to funded facilities and services and will prevent 'creaming' or the admission of only the 'more desirable clients', which can be a feature of some programmes. The measures include, *inter alia*:

- clear focus on target group;
- mandatory access for the target group;
- proof of the operation of strategies to attract the target group into the facility/programme; and
- integration with existing or proposed initiatives in the area.

Access for the target groups will be enforced where possible through the involvement of the local authorities and/or the VECs in the management structure. If this is not possible, then it will be necessary for projects to provide a satisfactory access programme showing how the target group will be reached and quantifying the extent of access.

Main Achievements of YPFSF

A speech by Minister of State for Local Development, and with special responsibility for the National Drugs Strategy, Mr Eoin Ryan, TD, at European Cities Against Drugs, Millennium Mayor's Conference, held in Cork, on 28 April 2000, overviewed achievements under the YPFSF. He stated, 'Through the Young People's Facilities and Services Fund, we are supporting the building or refurbishment of nearly fifty youth facilities, twenty sports clubs and nearly twenty community centres in disadvantaged areas. Almost eighty youth and outreach workers are being appointed to work with young people, offering them the type of developmental activities and educational programmes which were previously outside their reach, due to their family circumstances or their involvement with drugs or crime. The Fund is also supporting a wide variety of programmes, including early school leaving projects, family support programmes, art, drama and music, counselling and transport services.'

1.6.4 County/City Development Boards

Preliminary arrangements have been made to advance the objective of regional devolution, as outlined, for example, in the NDP (2000). Accordingly, the LDTFs and area-based partnership companies are to work with the newly-appointed Directors of Community and Enterprise and the County/City Development Boards (CDBs) when drawing up their integrated local action plans. Arrangements for co-ordination of planning and delivery of services are also to be agreed with the CDBs. It is likely that the YPFSF will adopt similar procedures when their next funding is due, i.e. 2002.

The recently-established County and City Development Boards (CDBs), whose primary function will be to draw up a comprehensive Strategy for Economic, Social and Cultural Development, by January 2002, have a key role in co-ordinating local delivery of Social Inclusion measures. The CDBs will operate on the partnership principle, with the Regional Assemblies and under the local government umbrella, with membership drawn from local development organisations, social partners, local representation of State agencies and local government itself (NDP, 2000). A Director of Community and Enterprise has been appointed by each CDB. All the relevant programmes and projects, and their delivery mechanisms, covered by the NDP, will be expected to accord with this framework.

1.6.5 Regional Health Boards

Responsibility for the provision of treatment and rehabilitation services for drug misusers throughout the country rests with the ten regional health boards. Each health board provides services in response to emerging trends in their own region, targeting specific segments of the local population and tailoring their services to the needs of their particular target groups.

With Government strategy beginning to address the drug problem on a nation-wide basis, in particular the use of recreational drugs, such as cannabis and ecstasy, particularly among young people, regional drugs co-ordinators have been appointed to assist the regional health boards in developing appropriate programmes and services, mostly in relation to drug awareness, education and prevention. The health boards have also set up regional co-ordinating committees in their areas, which work in partnership with other relevant agencies in developing a co-ordinated response to the drug problem, having regard to the needs of their particular regions. Under the National Drugs Strategy 2001-2008, Regional Drugs Task Forces are to be established in each of the health board areas, incorporating and expanding on the work of the regional co-ordinating committees (see Section 1.6.1 above).

The boards also provide support and training for community groups involved in drug-related prevention or rehabilitation activities.
Over 20 per cent of the actions identified in the National Drugs Strategy 2001-2008 (2001) are to be implemented by the regional health boards. The actions relate to the improved range and management of treatment and rehabilitation services.

In relation to range, health boards are to introduce a range of treatment and rehabilitation options as part of a planned programme of progression for each drug misuser by the end of 2002. These options are to be appropriate to the drug users' needs and circumstances and assist in their re-integration back into society. In addition, health boards are to explore the scope for provision of alternative and non-medical treatment types; oversee the development of comprehensive residential treatment models including detoxification, intervention, pre-treatment counselling, motivational work, therapeutic treatment and rehabilitation for misusers who wish to become drug-free; consider developing drop-in centres, respite facilities and half-way houses to help prevent relapse; and consider the feasibility of new suitably-trained peer-support groups to act as a rehabilitative support.

For drug misusers who are continuing to misuse, health boards are to review the existing network of needle-exchange facilities to ensure access for all injecting drug misusers to sterile injecting equipment. Moreover, they are to continue to develop good-practice outreach models, including models to outreach drug misusers who are not in contact with mainstream treatment or support agencies.

Standards for timeliness, volume and quality of service provision are all specified in the National Drugs Strategy 2001-2008. Drug misusers are to have immediate access to professional assessment and counselling by health board services, followed by commencement of treatment not later than one month after assessment. The number of treatment places for opiate addiction is to be increased to at least 6,500 by the end of 2002. In parallel, health boards are to consider how to increase the level of general practitioner and pharmacy involvement in primary treatment programmes, as a means of alleviating the pressure on the secondary treatment services. Health boards are to pursue the setting up of a Pilot Community Pharmacy Needle and Syringe Exchange programme in the ERHA area.

The quality of services to the drug misuser is to be enhanced. Well-publicised, short, easily-read guides to the drug treatment services available are to be distributed widely, with a view to enhancing access. Service-use charters specific to treatment and rehabilitation facilities will help ensure a greater balance in the relationship between the service provider and the service user. Moreover, treatment plans will be based on a 'continuum of care' model and a 'key worker' approach, which will provide a seamless transition between each different phase of treatment and after-care. To meet the needs of clients with parental responsibilities, health boards are to consider how best to integrate childcare facilities with treatment and rehabilitation centres and in residential treatment settings. Special consideration is given to the needs of young people, with the requirement to develop a protocol for the treatment of under 18 year olds presenting with serious drug problems; the provision of easy access to counselling services for young people seeking assistance with drug-related problems; and using means such as family therapy and community integration phases, to encourage family involvement in the treatment of young people.

Ensuring the long-term sustainability of the above actions, health boards are required to have in place by the end of 2002, a clearly co-ordinated and well publicised plan for the provision of a comprehensive and locally accessible range of treatments for drug users, particularly young people. This is to be implemented by the end of 2004. In conjunction with the production of this plan, health boards must develop a management plan in consultation with local communities to consider the location and establishment of treatment and rehabilitation facilities. Health boards are to report to the NACD on the efficacy of different forms of treatment and detox facilities and residential-drug free regimes on an ongoing basis, and all treatment providers are encouraged to co-operate in returning information on problem drug use to the National Drug Treatment Reporting System (NDTRS), managed by the Drug Misuse Research Division of the Health Research Board.

1.6.6 Community and Voluntary Sectors

The National Drugs Strategy Review Team 2001-2008 (2001) acknowledged the community and voluntary sectors as 'key actors' in the areas of drug supply reduction, prevention and treatment.

Through the LDTFs (see Section 1.6.2 above), local communities and voluntary organisations have participated in the planning, design and delivery of services The action plans of the LDTFs focus on developing community-based initiatives to link in with and add value to the programmes and services already being planned by the statutory agencies in the LDTF areas. Representatives of the two sectors are to sit on the proposed RDTFs as well. The National Drugs Strategy Review Team identified a need to strengthen and improve the level of community representation on task forces in order to ensure their effective engagement. However, the Review Team also warned that greater 'integration' might lead to greater 'formalisation', thereby alienating community groups themselves from their constituencies. The Strategy, therefore, recommends that the NDST consider funding, on a pilot basis, training initiatives to strengthen effective community representation and participation on Task Forces. The Strategy also recommends that the NDST examine the feasibility of introducing a standards and accreditation framework for all individuals, groups and agencies engaged in drug work.

The National Drugs Strategy 2001-2008 (2001) has identified a new community-based initiative in the area of prevention. RDTFs are to consider developing community-based initiatives to raise awareness. The goal of these initiatives would be to develop best-practice models, which send a clear and consistent message and which are capable of being mainstreamed. In the communities where drug misuse is most prevalent and where there is considerable knowledge about all aspects of the drugs issue, schools could tap into and use this knowledge as a beneficial aspect of their programmes.

The community and voluntary sectors participate in the development of drugs policy and drugs initiatives through a number of structures and consultative processes besides the LDTFs, as specified in the National Drugs Strategy 2001-

2008 (2001). Both sectors are represented on the NDST. They are to be increasingly involved in prison drug policy via the ongoing development of the Local Prison Liaison Groups and the formal meetings between the sectors and the Steering Group on Prison-Based Treatment Services. The Department of Justice, Equality and Law Reform is to consult with both the community sector and the Gardaí in establishing best-practice guidelines and approaches for community involvement in supply control activities, such as the Coastal Watch Programme. From 2002, regional health boards will be required to consult with local communities in developing a management plan for considering the location and establishment of treatment and rehabilitation facilities in local areas.

Structures exist to support community and voluntary groups working in the drugs area. The Department of Social, Community and Family Affairs funds the Dublin Citywide Drugs Crisis Campaign, a specialist support agency to its Community Development Support Programmes. The role of this support agency is to provide technical assistance and expertise to local communities to develop their capacity to respond to the drugs crisis in their areas and work alongside statutory and other agencies in tackling the problem at local level. As well as supporting local communities to develop skills to tackle the drug crisis, the agency also seeks to involve local communities in developing policies and making decisions on how resources are spent. The development of effective partnership relationships is key to this process.

The Voluntary Drug Treatment Network provides a framework for voluntary drug groups working in the area of treatment to meet, share issues of concern and develop more comprehensive responses to the prevention and treatment of problem drug use. The Network is an umbrella group that aims to challenge drug misuse and related issues in a creative, caring and motivational way. It is represented on the National AIDS Strategy Committee, NDST and NACD. However, the Network does not have a national remit to represent all voluntary drug treatment organisations in Ireland. It is mainly for Dublin-based organisations, which deal with drug misuse, but some of its members have a national focus in terms of treatment and training.

1.7 Evaluation of National Strategies

1.7.1 Social Inclusion and Evaluation of Drugs Initiatives

The policy frameworks underlying actions in the drugs area - the National Development Plan (NDP), National Anti-Poverty Strategy (NAPS) and Programme for Prosperity and Fairness (PPF) - are underpinned by a culture of evaluation and accountability. Thus, targets, review, evaluation, benchmarking and indicators are core concepts and, increasingly, resources are being set aside to develop the research capacity which can deliver good quality monitoring and evaluation (see Inter-Departmental Policy Committee, 1999- 2000). Poverty- and equality-proofing are also to become an integral aspect of national and regional programme development. The more general Social Inclusion initiatives in the drugs area, such as the LDTF and YPFSF, will be evaluated within this framework.

This culture of evaluation, however, is not as developed or formalised within drug treatment environments. Thus, few evaluations of treatment programmes have been conducted to date. However, the three-year research programme of the National Advisory Committee on Drugs (NACD) includes a number of evaluation studies in the drugs area, and regional health boards are increasingly adopting evidence-based approaches in their work and developing research and evaluation capabilities.

The implementation of Exchange of Drug Demand Reduction Action - EDDRA in Ireland by the Drug Misuse Research Division has also helped promote a culture of evaluation in the demand reduction context. Actors in the drugs area are aware that inclusion of projects in the EDDRA database requires such projects to have built-in evaluation. In addition, EDDRA training was made available to all regional drug co-ordinators by the DMRD, in collaboration with the EMCDDA. This training covered, *inter alia*, the planning and implementation of project evaluation and was evaluated highly by participants.

1.7.2 National Drugs Strategy 2001-2008

The National Drugs Strategy 2001-2008 includes a requirement for an evaluation framework. The strategy specifies:

- overall strategic objective;
- overall strategic aims;

- objectives under the four pillars of the strategy; and
- key performance indicators (KPIs) for the objectives.

The IDG, in conjunction with the NDST, is to establish an evaluation framework for the Strategy, focusing on the KPIs. Annual reports and mid-term evaluations, in 2004, will facilitate progress towards the key strategic goals. The cost-effectiveness of the various elements of each pillar of the new Strategy is to be established for the mid-term evaluation, to enable priorities to be reviewed and strategic objectives refocused if necessary.

Furthermore, evaluation is to be an integral stage in the implementation of the initiatives and programmes within each of the four pillars of the strategy. For example, the Irish Prisons Service is to commission an independent evaluation of the overall effectiveness of the Prison Strategy, to be carried out by mid 2004; the departments of Education and Science and Health and Children are to evaluate on an ongoing basis school-based education and preventative programmes; the Department of the Environment and Local Government is to commission an external evaluation of enforcement activity under the Housing Acts on homelessness, and also monitor and evaluate homelessness initiatives in relation to drugs issues. Agencies involved in service delivery, moreover, are to collect relevant data that will assist in evaluating programmes, e.g. recording and monitoring outputs, assembling best-practice guidelines, researching and establishing benchmarks.

1.7.3 Local Drugs Task Forces

The culture of evaluation outlined above ensures that evaluation is seen as an integral part of the planning exercises of the LDTFs. The Phase-2 updated plans were required to specify the proposed inputs and expected measurable outputs, outcomes and impacts in relation to each proposal and how it integrated into the overall drugs strategy. Thus, in addition to the evaluation of the overall process to measure its success or otherwise, evaluation of individual projects takes place with a view to mainstreaming those which are operating effectively (Department of Tourism, Sport and Recreation, 1999: 45).

In the handbook *Local Drugs Task Forces - A Local Response to the Drug Problem* (Department of Tourism, Sport and Recreation, 1999), the National Drugs Strategy Team names three mechanisms to facilitate the evaluation process:

- a steering group (comprising the National Drugs Strategy Team and the LDTFs) was set up to oversee and monitor the process;

- a specially-appointed evaluation co-ordinator devised terms of reference for the conduct of the evaluation, along with appropriate performance indicators and these were approved by the steering group; and

- a panel of evaluators was formed. LDTFs were free to nominate persons or companies to this panel, provided they met the criteria outlined above. LDTFs could then make their selection of evaluators from the approved panel. In the event of there being excessive demand for the services of particular evaluators, the steering group determined their assignment.

The handbook also states that the evaluation process must be objective and transparent, and must be carried out by individuals with a recognised and proven track record, in accordance with agreed criteria.

Evaluation Criteria for LDTF Projects
Over 200 projects were approved for funding on foot of the initial LDTF plans. There was a wide variation in range, type and size of projects. From a financial viewpoint, projects were divided into three types: those costing over Ir£50,000 / €63,487 per annum; those costing between Ir£10,000 / €12,700 and Ir£50,000 / €63,487 per annum; and those costing less than Ir£10,000 / €12,700 per annum. The majority of projects were set up with a view to being ongoing, but some were once-off.

Acknowledging the wide variety of projects (including the fact that they address the drug problem under different themes, e.g. education/prevention, treatment, rehabilitation, and community policing/estate management), it was acknowledged that it would be difficult to devise one evaluation framework that would suit all projects. It was recommended to develop a process that could be applied in a flexible manner, depending on the type of project. It was envisaged that more rigorous evaluations would take place with the more expensive projects.

Guidelines as to how the evaluations were to be carried out, along with the ground rules, were considered necessary and were developed by the steering group, in consultation with the evaluation co-ordinator, LDTFs and project promoters as the process developed.

As reported above, 140 LDTF projects were evaluated in April-June 2000, and 122 of these were mainstreamed. PR Consultancy co-ordinated a composite report on the evaluation.

1.7.4 Young People's Facilities and Services Fund

An overall evaluation of the YPFSF is to be undertaken in 2001. The evaluation will be based on good practice as established by preceding evaluation mechanisms, e.g. mechanisms for the LDTF and the mainstreaming of youth service projects.

1.8 Conclusions

Ireland's National Drugs Strategy 2001-2008 has been developed in the context of various international and EU agreements, for example the Political Declaration on the Guiding Principles of Drugs Demand Reduction (UN Special Session on Drugs, held in New York, 1998),[8] the UN Conventions on Narcotic Drugs and Psychotropic Substances,[9] the EU Action Plan on Drugs 2000 - 2004 (Commission of the European Communities, 1999), and the EU Drugs Strategy 2000 - 2004 (CORDROGUE 64, 1999). Development of the strategy has also involved extensive consultation, including public fora in a number of centres throughout the country.

The main changes and new directions in Irish drugs policy, strategies, implementation and evaluation can be summarised as follows:

---

[8] At a UN Special Session on Drugs, held in New York in 1998, a Political Declaration on the Guiding Principles of Drug Demand Reduction was adopted. It put an onus on every member state to have in place a comprehensive drugs policy and an outline of how targets are to be achieved over the period 2000 to 2008.

[9] Single Convention on Narcotic Drugs, 1961, as amended by the 1972 Protocol Amending the Single Convention on Narcotic Drugs, 1961; the Convention on Psychotropic Substances, 1971; and the UN Convention against the Illicit Traffic in Narcotic Drugs and Psychotropic Substances, 1988. The conventions may be accessed through the website - www.incb.org/e/conv/

- publication of a major review of the National Drugs Strategy;
- adoption of the promotion of Social Inclusion as one of the priorities of the National Development Plan 2000-2006, and the situation of the drugs issue within this context;
- adoption of National Drugs Strategy for 2001-2008 (2001);
- greater devolution of power to regional structures, with which existing structures in the drugs area will co-operate;
- continued adoption of an integrated, inter-agency response to the drugs problem involving local communities;
- continued involvement of local communities in the development and implementation of drugs policy;
- increasing role of voluntary and community sectors;
- continued development of a culture of evaluation and increased resources of knowledge infrastructure to support same; and
- development of drug-related research and information capability.

1.9 References

Commission of the European Communities (COM) (1999). *Communication from the Commission to the Council and the European Parliament on a European Action Plan to Combat Drugs 2000-2004.* COM (99) 239 Final.

CORDROGUE 64 (1999). *European Union Drug Strategy 2000-2004.* 12555/3/99 REV 3. COREPER document to the Council/European Council.

Department of Health and Children (2000). *The National Health Promotion Strategy 2000 - 2005.* Dublin: Department of Health and Children.

Department of Tourism, Sport and Recreation (1999). *Local Drugs Task Forces, A Local Response to the Drug Problem, Handbook.* Dublin: Department of Tourism, Sport and Recreation.

Department of Tourism, Sport and Recreation (2001). *Building on Experience: National drugs strategy 2001-2008.* Dublin: The Stationery Office.
Drug Misuse Research Division (1999). *National Report on Drug Issues: Ireland 1999. Report for EMCDDA.* Internal Document, Dublin: Drug Misuse Research Division, Health Research Board.

Eastern Health Board (1998). *AIDS/Drug Addiction Services: Inventory of policies.* Dublin: Eastern Health Board.

Flood, C. (1999). Address by Mr Christopher Flood, at press conference to announce the allocation of funding under the Young People's Facilities and Services Fund in the 13 Drug Task Force Areas, Monday 26 April 1999, Dublin. Unpublished.

An Garda Síochána (1999). *Annual Report of An Garda Síochána 1998.* Dublin: The Stationery Office.

Inter-Departmental Committee (1998-1999). *Social Inclusion Strategy, National Anti-Poverty Strategy. Annual Report.* Dublin: The Stationery Office.

Inter-Departmental Committee (1999-2000). *Social Inclusion Strategy, National Anti-Poverty Strategy. Annual Report.* Dublin: Brunswick Press Ltd.

Irish Prisons Service (2000). *Report of the Steering Group on Prison Based Drug Treatment Services.* Dublin: Irish Prisons Service.

Ministerial Task Force on Measures to Reduce the Demand for Drugs (1996). *First Report.* Dublin: Department of the Taoiseach.

Ministerial Task Force on Measures to Reduce the Demand for Drugs (1997). *Second Report.* Dublin: Department of the Taoiseach.

Moran, R., O'Brien, M., Dillon, L. & Farrell, E., with Mayock, P. (2001). *Overview of Drug Issues in Ireland 2000: A Resource Document.* Dublin: The Health Research Board.

National Drugs Strategy (2001). *Ireland's National Drugs Strategy 2001-2008.* Dublin: The Stationery Office.

NAPS (National Anti-Poverty Strategy) (1998/99; 1999/2000). *National Anti-Poverty Strategy.* Dublin: Government Publications.
NDP (National Development Plan) (2000). *Ireland, National Development Plan 2000-2006.* Dublin: The Stationery Office.

O'Brien, M. & Moran, R. (1998). *National Report on Drugs Issues Ireland 1998.* Internal Document. Dublin: Drug Misuse Research Division, The Health Research Division.

Office of the Revenue Commissioners (1993). *The Revenue Commissioners Annual Report 1992.* Dublin: The Stationery Office.

PA Consulting Group (1998). *Evaluation of Drugs Initiative.* Dublin: Department of Tourism, Sport and Recreation.

PPF (Programme for Prosperity and Fairness) (2000). *Programme for Prosperity and Fairness.* Dublin: The Stationery Office.

Chapter 2

Drug-Related Infectious Diseases

Lucy Dillon and Mary O'Brien

2.1 Introduction

As in other European countries, the advent of HIV/AIDS and the connection made between its spread and injecting drug use, can be seen to have played a key role in influencing the development of drug-related policy and services in Ireland (Butler, 1991; O'Gorman, 1998). Prior to the early 1990s, abstinence was seen as the most acceptable goal for Irish drug-treatment programmes. However, the early 1990s saw a move toward greater use of harm-reduction strategies and the expansion of substitution and needle exchange programmes in Irish drug-treatment services. The 1991 Government Strategy to Prevent Drug Misuse confirmed both the shift in treatment philosophy from one based solely on abstinence to one that included a harm-reduction strategy, and the central role the advent of HIV had played in this policy shift:

> Insofar as HIV infection is concerned, of the 1,049 cases identified, 582 (or 57%) are drug misuse related. … It is clear from the foregoing that the prevention of transmission of HIV virus in this country must include strategies developed to deal with the drug misuse problem. …These strategies must be community based, client orientated and, given the serious nature of the problem, of necessity, innovative. They must include emphasis on outreach programmes involving counselling, methadone maintenance and needle exchange. Advice on risk reduction services generally must form an essential part of any such strategies to minimise the spread of the disease [HIV/AIDS]; (*Government Strategy to Prevent Drug Misuse*, 1991: 7).

Furthermore, while the two reports produced by the Ministerial Task Force to Reduce the Demand for Drugs (1996, 1997) continued to reiterate the ultimate aim of all treatment programmes as abstinence, harm-minimisation strategies, specifically aimed at preventing the spread of HIV (i.e. substitution and needle exchange programmes), became a central feature of drug-treatment services. The second report of the Task Force argued that it had developed 'a strong philosophy of harm reduction and treatment of the consequences of drug abuse - stabilisation, methadone maintenance, detoxification, rehabilitation and re-integration' (Ministerial Task Force to Reduce the Demand for Drugs, 1997: 7).

While HIV/AIDS may be seen as the drug-related infectious disease that was at the centre of drug policy development in Ireland, other diseases, in particular hepatitis C, are attracting an increasing amount of attention from those working in the area. The following sections of this chapter will address three key issues on drug-related infectious diseases in the Irish context:

> 2.2 Prevalence of HIV, HBV and HCV among Drug Users
> 2.3 Determinants of Drug-Related Infectious Diseases
> 2.4 Consequences of Drug-Related Infectious Diseases
> 2.5 New Developments and Uptake of Prevention/Harm Reduction and Care

2.2 Prevalence of HIV, HBV and HCV among Drug Users

Epidemiological analysis of drug-related infectious diseases in Ireland is somewhat restricted by a lack of data. The gap in information is particularly acute in relation to hepatitis B and C. The following sections will examine the data that are available in relation to each of the relevant drug-related infectious diseases: HIV, hepatitis B and hepatitis C.

2.2.1 HIV
The majority of data collected on drug-related infectious diseases are related to HIV. There are two main sources of data that will be discussed below: first, the routine data on HIV-positive tests reported by the Department of Health and Children; and second, special studies that have estimated the prevalence of HIV among particular cohorts of drug users.

Routine Data on HIV Testing

In Ireland, at the time of writing, the Department of Health and Children, in collaboration with the Virus Reference Laboratory, based in University College, Dublin, produces statistics on HIV-positive tests, which are published every six months. The figures relating to HIV tests are broken down according to risk category. There are a number of risk categories identified in relation to HIV infection, including injecting drug use, homosexual sex and haemophiliac contact. Therefore, it is possible to get a breakdown of the number of positive HIV cases attributable to injecting drug use in a given year. However, there are a number of limitations to this data source that should be noted:

- it is limited to the tested population. Nothing can be inferred for those drug users who have not been tested;
- it is not possible to identify non-injecting drug users within the data set;
- no socio-demographic data are collected on those who are tested;
- there is only a limited geographical breakdown available;
- a gender breakdown has only been made available since 1997; and
- both risk behaviours (e.g. injecting drug use) and test locations (e.g. prison) are used as categories. This makes the data somewhat unclear. For example, it is not known through what risk activity those tested in the prison setting became infected with HIV.

Despite these limitations, this data source provides the best information with which to examine the epidemiological profile of HIV in Ireland over the past decade and a half.

The cumulative figures for the positive cases of HIV from the start of data collection in 1982 up until 1985, show that just over 60 per cent (n=221) of all positive cases (n=363) were attributed to injecting drug use (see Table 2.1). Since 1985, injecting drug use has continued to be one of the main risk categories, accounting for 41.6 per cent of the cumulative number of positive cases up until 31 December 1999 (see Table 2.1). Two possible explanations have been given by O'Gorman (1999) for the high proportion of intravenous drug users in the known HIV-positive population. She argues that the culture of injecting drug use that existed among drug users in Ireland during the 1980s, at a time when both information on safe injecting practices and access to clean injecting equipment were limited,[1] resulted in the rapid transmission of HIV among the injecting

---

1 The first needle exchange programme in Dublin was established in 1989.

population. Secondly, she argues, the injecting drug-using population may be more likely to have been tested for HIV through their contact with drug-treatment services than those individuals who may be at risk of infection through other routes, e.g. heterosexual sex (O'Gorman, 1999: 6).

TABLE 2.1
Ireland 1985–1999. HIV-Positive Cases by Risk Category.
Numbers and Percentages.

Year	IDUs*		Homosexual Sex		Heterosexual Sex / Risk Unspecified		Other		TOTAL	
	n	%	n	(%)	n	(%)	n	(%)	n	(%)
1985**	221	(60.9)	39	(10.7)	0		103	(28.4)	363	(100.0)
1986	112	(66.3)	11	(6.5)	21	(12.5)	25	(14.8)	169	(100.0)
1987	72	(49.7)	21	(14.5)	26	(17.9)	26	(17.9)	145	(100.0)
1988	58	(50.4)	17	(14.8)	20	(17.4)	20	(17.4)	115	(100.0)
1989	57	(49.1)	33	(28.5)	0		26	(22.4)	116	(100.0)
1990	50	(45.1)	25	(22.5)	24	(21.6)	12	(10.8)	111	(100.0)
1991	34	(36.9)	27	(29.4)	25	(27.2)	6	(6.5)	92	(100.0)
1992	82	(40.8)	58	(28.9)	50	(24.9)	11	(5.5)	201	(100.1)
1993	52	(38.0)	48	(35.0)	21	(15.3)	16	(11.7)	137	(100.0)
1994	20	(23.5)	31	(36.5)	22	(25.9)	12	(14.1)	85	(100.0)
1995	19	(20.9)	33	(36.3)	30	(33.0)	9	(9.9)	91	(100.1)
1996	20	(18.9)	41	(38.7)	27	(25.5)	18	(17.0)	106	(100.1)
1997	21	(17.7)	37	(31.1)	40	(33.6)	21	(17.7)	119	(100.1)
1998	26	(19.1)	37	(27.2)	47	(34.6)	26	(19.1)	136	(100.0)
1999	69	(33.0)	40	(19.1)	59	(28.2)	41	(19.6)	209	(99.9)
Total	913	(41.6)	498	(22.7)	412	(18.8)	372	(17.0)	2,195	(100.1)

Source: Department of Health and Children.
* IDUs = Intravenous drug users.
** Cumulative figure for 1982–5.

The proportion of positive cases attributed to the intravenous drug user category generally decreased from 1992 through to 1998. In 1994, for the first time, intravenous drug use accounted for fewer new positive cases than the 'homosexual sex' or 'heterosexual sex/risk unspecified' categories (see Table 2.1). In fact, the proportion of positive HIV tests attributed to intravenous drug use fell from 49.1 per cent in 1989, to a low of 17.7 per cent in 1997 (see Table 2.1). It is suggested that the reduction, both proportionately and in absolute numbers, over this period may be attributed, at least in part, to the expansion of services aimed at reducing the spread of HIV among injecting drug users, i.e. substitution and needle exchange programmes. In an analysis of the trends up until 1998 the National AIDS Strategy Committee comments that:

> Epidemiological surveillance of HIV would indicate that in recent years the overall incidence of HIV among intravenous drug users is reducing. While we must be wary of drawing major conclusions from short term changes in infection patterns service providers are optimistic that this trend is as a result of the intervention through a combination of substitution therapy with methadone and needle exchange service (National AIDS Strategy Committee, 2000: 63).

Despite the apparent reduction in the proportion of the total number of positive cases attributed to injecting drug use, figures from 1999 show a substantial increase in the number of positive cases attributed to injecting drug use. Between 1998 and 1999 the total number of new cases of HIV increased from 136 to 209. Furthermore, the number of new positive cases attributed to injecting drug use increased from 26 of the total new cases (n=136) in 1998, to 69 of the new cases (n=209) in 1999. Therefore, proportionately, injecting drug use as a risk category increased from accounting for 19.1 per cent of new HIV-positive cases within this data source in 1998, to 33 per cent in 1999. This is the highest annual proportion of new positive cases attributed to injecting drug use since 1993.

Anecdotal evidence suggests a couple of explanations for the increase in the number of positive cases attributable to injecting drug use during 1999. Firstly, leading on from the Protocol for the Prescribing of Methadone, issued by the Department of Health (1993), guidelines were developed for general practitioners prescribing methadone within the general-practice setting and for pharmacists in their dispensing of methadone. Following the completion and evaluation of a pilot programme, the Report of the Methadone Treatment Services Review Group made a number of recommendations on tightening control on both the prescribing and dispensing of methadone, in accordance with the 1993 protocol (Department of Health, 1997). Consequently, the Misuse of Drugs (Supervision of Prescription and Supply of Methadone) Regulations were drawn up in 1998. The regulations aim to create a more controlled environment for the prescribing and dispensing of methadone. Within this context, all those who were receiving methadone in Ireland were integrated into a structured programme. Furthermore, drug users were integrated into a structured programme-setting, where there is an active policy of carrying out virology (blood test) in relation to HIV and hepatitis. It is suggested that this may have resulted in an increase in the number of injecting drug users being tested for HIV and, in turn, an increase in the number of positive cases being attributed to injecting drug use during 1999. Secondly, it has been suggested anecdotally that perceptions may be beginning to change among the drug-using population in relation to HIV. It is argued that the availability of new treatment, i.e. Highly Active Anti-Retroviral Treatment (HAART), and the visibility of individuals in the community for whom treatment has been effective, has encouraged people to come forward for testing so that they can avail of treatment if necessary.

HIV among Prisoners
As mentioned above, within the Department of Health and Children's reporting system on HIV-positive tests, those who are tested in prison are categorised according to the testing location, i.e. prison. Although the proportion of positive cases from the testing location category of prison which are attributable to injecting drug use is not known, anecdotal evidence suggests that most of those being tested have a history of injecting drug use. Since 1989, a total of thirty-nine new positive cases have been attributed to 'prisoners', thirteen of whom tested positive in 1999. The use of both risk categories and testing locations in the Department of Health and Children's reporting system does not allow for any conclusions to be drawn as to the significance of these figures in relation to the injecting drug-using population. It is important that the risk category of these cases be clarified.

HIV and Gender
Gender is the only socio-demographic data collected from those who are tested for HIV by the Department of Health and Children. Gender has been reported since 1997. An examination of the figures by gender suggests a possible change in the profile of those who are testing positive for HIV in Ireland (see Table 2.2). In 1997, females only accounted for three of the twenty-one new positive cases

attributed to injecting drug use. In 1998 this had increased to ten of the twenty-six positive cases among injecting drug users, and in 1999 it had increased further to account for thirty-four of the sixty-nine positive cases. Speaking in percentage terms, women have increased from representing 14.3 per cent of the positive tests among injecting drug users in 1997, to 38 per cent in 1998, to 49 per cent in 1999. Owing to the lack of information on gender prior to 1997, it is not possible to explore trends over a more extended period of time. Anecdotal evidence suggests that these figures may reflect a real increase in the number of female,   injecting drug-users who are becoming infected with HIV. However, it is also suggested that these women may be becoming infected through their sexual behaviour rather than their injecting drug use. Once identified as an injecting drug user, however, their infection will tend to be attributed to their injecting drug-using behaviour. Anecdotal evidence also suggests that a growing number of women may be attending for testing in order to be able to minimise the risk of infection to their baby were they to become pregnant.

TABLE 2.2
Ireland 1997–1999. HIV Sero-Positive Intravenous Drug Users by Gender.
Numbers and Percentages.

Year	Male		Female		Total	
	n	%	n	%	n	%
1997	18	(85.7)	3	(14.3)	21	(100)
1998	16	(61.5)	10	(38.5)	26	(100)
1999	35	(50.7)	34	(49.3)	69	(100)

Source: Department of Health and Children.

Special Studies on HIV Prevalence
A number of special studies have been carried out, which have explored the prevalence of HIV among cohorts of drug users in a range of study locations. The studies include drug users located in: the community, drug-treatment centres, needle exchange programmes and prisons. A summary of the research findings on the prevalence of HIV infection among particular cohorts of drug users is presented in Table 2.3 below.

One of the first studies of drug use in Dublin began in 1985, when O'Kelly & Bury (1996) identified a cohort of known intravenous drug users in an inner city area. The prevalence of HIV infection among this group was monitored over the next decade. In 1991, 57.3 per cent of the total cohort (n=82) were known to be

HIV positive; by 1994, 64.6 per cent of the cohort had tested positive for HIV. In total, eighteen of those who had tested positive by 1994 had died. O'Kelly & Bury (1996) argue that the high prevalence rate of HIV among this cohort reflects the context in which their intravenous drug use developed. They argue that 'the uncontrolled use of injected drugs and the sharing of scarce equipment were commonplace at the time; the true impact of these practices is now clear in terms of the spread of HIV infection among the young people who lived there' (O'Kelly & Bury, 1996: 114). Another study, carried out in Dublin with a cohort who had begun injecting during the same period, found similar rates of HIV prevalence. Williams, Mullan, O'Connor & Kinsella (1990) found that, of a cohort of sixty-nine individuals on a methadone maintenance programme, 70 per cent were HIV positive.

These high prevalence rates of HIV were not found in the Dublin-based studies subsequent to those of O'Kelly & Bury (1996) and Williams *et al.* (1990). Johnson *et al.* (1994) found that in 1991, 14.8 per cent of a sample recruited from a needle exchange programme were HIV positive. The Dorman, Keenan, Schuttler, Merry & O'Connor (1997) study, carried out in 1992 in the context of a World Health Organisation multi-national research initiative, found that 8.4 per cent of a sample of 180 injecting drug users, recruited from both in and out of treatment, were HIV positive. In contrast, the Smyth, Keenan & O'Connor (1998) study of a drug-treatment sample, tested between 1992 and 1997, found a prevalence rate for HIV of only 1.2 per cent. This is low in contrast to an estimated 8 per cent prevalence rate (based on laboratory reports) among injectors attending Eastern Health Board methadone clinics in 1997 (Barry, cited in Allwright, Barry, Bradley, Long & Thornton, 1999: 2).

More recently, two studies have been carried, reporting on HIV prevalence among the Irish prison population (Allwright et al., 1999; Long *et al.*, 2000). Included in the data are the prevalence rates for those prisoners who have a history of injecting drug use. It was found that 5.8 per cent of committal prisoners[2] (Long et al., 2000) and 3.5 per cent of general prisoners[3] (Allwright et al., 1999) with a history of injecting drug use were HIV positive. Among those prisoners who reported no history of injecting drug use, the infection rates were 0.5 per cent among the committal population (Long et al., 2000) and 0.9 per cent within the general prison population (Allwright et al., 1999). In an environment where injecting drug use is on-going, and in the absence of any provision for clean injecting equipment, the risk for the spread of infection within this population is high.

In summary, injecting drug use continues to be one of the main risk categories to which HIV-positive cases are attributed each year. Despite the rate of new HIV-positive cases attributed to injecting drug use plateauing in the early and mid-1990s, recent figures suggest that there is an upward trend in the number of new HIV-positive cases among Irish drug users. The information available on those testing positive for HIV remains limited. Analysis of the figures highlights the need for more information, in particular of a socio-demographic and behavioural nature, to facilitate comprehensive epidemiological analysis of the trends.

Table 2.3. Ireland 1994-1999. Summary of Research Findings on the Prevalence of HIV Infection among Particular Cohorts of Drug Users.

Author	Study Period	Sample Source	Self Report/ Test	Serum/ Saliva	Sample Size Tested	% Infected of Those Tested
Long et al., (2000)	1999	Committal Prisoners n=593	Test	Saliva	IDUs [4] (n=173)	IDUs 5.8%
Allwright et al., (1999)	1998	Irish Prisoners n= 1,178	Test	Saliva	IDUs (n=509)	IDUs 3.5%
Smyth et al., (1998)	1992-1997	Drug Treatment Centre n=735	Test	Serum	IDUs (n=600)	IDUs 1.2%
Dorman et. al., (1997)	1992	Drug Treatment Centre & Non-Treatment n=185	Test	Serum and saliva	IDUs (n=180)	IDUs 8.4%
O'Kelly et. al., (1996)	1984-1995	IDUs in community n=82	Test	Serum	IDUs (n=66)	IDUs 65%
Johnson et al., (1994)	1991	Needle Exchange	Test	Saliva	IDUs (n=81)	IDUs 14.8%

[2] 'Committal prisoners are prisoners who have been admitted to the prison within the preceding 48 hours, accused or guilty of a new crime, excluding those on temporary release or transferred from another prison. The committal population includes individuals entering on remand, following sentence, committed as a result of a bench warrant and non-nationals without valid documentation' (Long et al., 2000: 2).
[3] All those incarcerated irrespective of their committal status.
[4] IDUs: Injecting drug users

2.2.2 Hepatitis B

There is very little information in Ireland on the prevalence and incidence of hepatitis B among both the general population and the injecting drug-using population. While data are collected on the number of positive tests carried out for hepatitis B by the Virus Reference Laboratory, no behavioural data are collected and, therefore, those infected through drug use cannot be identified. Information on prevalence rates is thus confined to a small number of special studies that have been carried out in the field.

The Smyth et al. (1998) study of drug users located in a treatment setting found that only 1 per cent were infected with hepatitis B. However, more recent research carried out in the prison setting found significantly higher prevalence rates among injecting drug users. Allwright et al. (1999) and Long et al. (2000) found 18.5 per cent and 17.9 per cent prevalence rates for hepatitis B, respectively. While these figures suggest that hepatitis B may be prevalent among the injecting drug-user population, the lack of data prohibits any in-depth epidemiological analysis of the situation in Ireland.

TABLE 2.4

Ireland 1998-2000. Summary of Research Findings on the Prevalence of Hepatitis B Infection among Particular Cohorts of Drug Users.

Numbers and Percentages.

Author	Study Period	Sample Source	Self Report Test	Serum/Saliva	Sample Size Tested	%Infected of Those Tested
Long *et al.*, (2000)	1999	Committal Prisoners n=593	Test	Saliva	IDUs (n=173)	IDUs 17.9%
Allwright *et al.*, (1999)	1998	Irish Prison Population n=1,178	Test	Saliva	IDUs (n=509)	IDUs 18.5%
Smyth *et al.*, (1998)	1992-1997	Drug Treatment Centre n=735	Test	Serum	IDUs (n=729)	IDUs 1%

IDUs = Intravenous drug users.

2.2.3 Hepatitis C

In Ireland, there is no routine data collection in the area of hepatitis C. However, there have been a number of special studies carried out among samples of drug users in a variety of study settings (see Table 2.5).

The first study of hepatitis C infection among injecting drug-users was carried out between August 1992 and August 1993 by Smyth, Keenan, Dorman & O'Connor (1995). The study sample was identified through a treatment centre, where all new attenders and re-attenders who presented during the study period and who reported a history of injecting drug use were encouraged to take part. In total, 272 injecting drug-users took part and a prevalence rate of 84 per cent for infection with hepatitis C was found. Among those injectors who had been injecting for between six months and two years inclusive, the prevalence rate was 70 per cent. Among those with an injecting history of longer than two years, the prevalence rate was 95 per cent. Furthermore, there was a significant gender difference in relation to infection: of the 194 males, 156 (80%) tested positive, whereas 73 of the 78 females (94%) were positive.

Further studies were carried out by Smyth et al. (1998) and Smyth, Keenan & O'Connor (1999a), which examined the prevalence of hepatitis C infection among in-treatment populations. Consecutive new attenders at a treatment service, who attended between July 1993 and December 1996, were approached to take part in the study. In all, a sample of 353 injecting drug-users who reported an injecting history of less than twenty-five months were recruited. Overall, a prevalence rate of 52.1 per cent was recorded in this sample. In an extension of this study cohort, Smyth et al. (1998) later found that of 733 consecutive new attenders between September 1992 and September 1997 at the same treatment centre, 61.8 per cent were hepatitis C positive.

In two prison studies, which have been discussed in previous sections, the prevalence of hepatitis C among prisoners was explored (Allwright et al., 1999; Long et al., 2000). The prevalence of hepatitis C infection was found to be high within this population. Allwright et al. (1999) found that among 509 prisoners with a history of injecting drug use, 81.3 per cent tested positive for hepatitis C. In contrast, only 3.7 per cent of those prisoners who did not report a history of injecting drug use had tested positive for hepatitis C. A follow-up study of the committal prisoner population (Long et al., 2000) found that, of 173 prisoners with a history of injecting drug use, 71.7 per cent were hepatitis C positive. Only

1.4 per cent of those prisoners who reported that they had no history of injecting drug use tested positive for hepatitis C.

TABLE 2.5

Ireland 1995-2000 Summary of Research Findings on the Prevalence of Hepatitis C Infection among Particular Cohorts of Drug Users.

Numbers and Percentages.

Author	Testing Period	Sample Source	Self Report Test	Serum/ Saliva	Sample Size Tested	%Infected of Those Tested
Long *et al.,* (2000)	1999	Committal Prisoners n=593	Test	Serum	IDUs (n=173) Non IDUs (n=420)	IDUs 71.7% Non IDUs 1.4%
Allwright *et al.,* (1999)	1998	Irish Prison Population n=1,178	Test	Serum	IDUs (n=509) Non IDUs (n=669)	IDUs 81.3% Non IDUs 3.7%
Smyth *et al.,* (1998)	1993-1996	Drug Treatment Centre n=353	Test	Serum	IDUs (n=353)	IDUs 52.1%
Smyth *et al.,* (1999b)	1997	Drug Treatment Centre n=84	Self-report	n/a	IDUs (n=84)	IDUs 89%
Smyth *et al.,* (1998)	1992-1997	Drug Treatment Centre n=735	Test	Serum	IDUs (n=733)	IDUs 61.8%
Smyth *et al.,* (1995)	1992-1993	Drug Treatment Centre n=272	Test	Serum	IDUs (n=272)	IDUs 84%

IDUs = Intravenous drug users.

While it is not possible from the available data to analyse infection trends over time, it would appear from the studies available that hepatitis C infection has been prevalent among Irish injecting drug-users over the past decade. Anecdotal evidence suggests that the relative ease with which hepatitis C can be spread through injecting drug use, and a lack of knowledge among users about hepatitis C and the associated risks, have all contributed to its spread. In summary, the prevalence rate for hepatitis C infection has been found to be consistently high within the drug-using population over the past decade.

2.2.4 Summary

The most comprehensive data available on drug-related infectious diseases in Ireland are for HIV. While the number of new, positive tested cases for HIV, which were attributable to injecting drug use, appeared to stabilise in the mid-1990s, figures for 1999 show an increase in the number of cases. For both hepatitis B and C, analysis is dependent solely on data from special studies. Despite the absence of comprehensive data it appears from the evidence available that hepatitis C continues to be highly prevalent among Irish injecting drug users. Overall, it would appear from the data available that drug-related infectious diseases continue to be a concern in relation to Irish injecting drug users. Furthermore, this highlights the need for more comprehensive data collection in the area of all drug-related infectious diseases in order to monitor changes in the trends over time.

2. 3 Determinants of Drug-Related Infectious Diseases

This section addresses some of the determinants of drug-related infectious diseases in the Irish context. It examines research that has looked at the risk behaviours engaged in by Irish drug users, both in relation to their injecting drug use and their sexual behaviour. Furthermore, it explores the data available on both the health-related consequences and the wider social consequences of drug-related infectious diseases.

2.3.1 Injecting Risk Behaviour

Once the link between the spread of HIV and injecting drug use was established in the mid-1980s, the risk behaviours engaged in by the injecting drug-using population became a focus of research. In the Irish context, studies on the injecting risk behaviour of drug users have spanned the last decade. During this period the provision of harm-reduction strategies has expanded from being available through a small number of programmes to a small number of drug users, to more widespread availability, to a significant number of programmes catering for a significant number of drug users. This section first describes the findings of research related to the risk behaviours of the general injecting population, and then second describes the findings relating to three sub-groups of particular interest - young injectors, female injectors and injecting drug users in prison.

Injecting Drug Users in General

Research carried out by Johnson et al. (1994) in 1991, among a sample of attendees at a Dublin needle exchange, found that 52.6 per cent of respondents reported that they had not shared equipment during the preceding twenty-eight days, while over 34.2 per cent had shared with two or more other people. A study carried out a year later, in 1992 (Dorman et al., 1997), among a sample (n=185) of injecting drug users both in and out of treatment, found that 55.7 per cent of the sample had shared and 61.6 per cent had lent injecting equipment in the previous six months.

Despite the expansion of harm-reduction strategies since the two studies described above (Johnson et al., 1994; Dorman et al., 1997) were carried out, more recent research has found that Irish drug users continue to engage in risky injecting behaviour. In a study of those attending a needle exchange programme, Cox & Lawless (2000) found that 59 per cent of the sample who had a history of injecting drug use (n=1,323) reported sharing injecting equipment at some stage in their injecting drug-using career. Furthermore, 29 per cent of these respondents reported sharing recently (i.e. in the previous four weeks). Among the 29 per cent who reported sharing recently, 17 per cent had lent their injecting equipment, 50 per cent had borrowed it and 33 per cent had done both. Data from the National Drug Treatment Reporting System (NDTRS), operated by the Drug Misuse Research Division of the Health Research Board, offers further evidence that Irish drug users continue to engage in injecting risk behaviours. In 1998, 575 out of first-treatment contacts (n=1,625) reported that they had ever injected a drug, and 45.6 per cent of these reported that they had ever shared injecting equipment. Furthermore, 352 of this sample reported that they were currently injecting (i.e. within the last month), and 26 per cent (n=94) of these reported that they were currently sharing injecting equipment (i.e. within the last month).

Young Injectors

In a study specifically aimed at exploring the risk behaviours engaged in by a sample of young injectors (n=485), i.e. those under the age of 25, Cassin, Geoghegan & Cox (1998) found a significant proportion regularly engaged in injecting risk behaviours. Compared with a cohort of older injectors (n=285), i.e. those over the age of 25, who were attending the same service, younger clients were found to be significantly more likely to have reported both lending and borrowing used needles and syringes in the four weeks prior to first contact with the syringe exchange programme. Furthermore, 64.3 per cent of the younger cohort reported that they had shared injecting paraphernalia (i.e. spoons and filters) in the four weeks prior to contacting the service, compared to only 43.8 per cent of the older cohort.

Female Injectors

Female drug users have been studied specifically in relation to their injecting risk behaviours. Cox & Lawless (2000) found that among a cohort of needle-exchange clients, women (n=304) were significantly more likely than men (n=1,000) to report sharing injecting equipment with their sexual partner and to share injecting paraphernalia with other injecting drug users. While 53 per cent of men reported that they had shared injecting paraphernalia, 63 per cent of females reported that they did so. The gender difference was more acute in relation to sharing injecting equipment with a sexual partner: 13 per cent of men compared to 37 per cent of women reported that they did so. However, this was directly related to the fact that 68 per cent of women reported that they had a sexual partner who was an injecting drug user, compared to just 24 per cent of men. Cox & Lawless (2000) argue that the greater personal involvement of women with other drug users has consequences in terms of health-related problems and risk behaviour. The social opportunities created by living in close proximity with other injecting drug users creates an environment in which risk behaviour flourishes (Cox & Lawless, 2000).

Injecting Drug Users in Prison

To date, Irish prisoners do not have access to clean injecting equipment and only a very limited number have access to a methadone maintenance programme in the prison setting. This implies that, where injecting drug use occurs in the prison, it may be particularly risky in relation to the spread of drug-related infectious diseases.

O'Mahony's (1997) study in a Dublin prison found that 42 per cent (n=45) of a sample of 108 prisoners had used heroin while in prison serving their current sentence. Of these forty-five, thirty-seven had engaged in intravenous use. One-sixth of those reporting a history of drug use had tested positive for HIV, while a quarter had never been tested. In addition, half these drug users said they had tested positive for at least one form of hepatitis. O'Mahony described as 'alarming' (O'Mahony, 1997: 107) the finding that, of those who reported having tested positive for HIV, 60 per cent had engaged in needle sharing since being notified of their positive status. An earlier study, based on data gathered between 1987 and 1991, found that during this period, 168 known HIV-positive prisoners had spent time in Mountjoy Prison in Dublin. A study of a sub-sample of these HIV-positive individuals, selected on a random basis, found that 94 per cent had engaged in drug use within the prison, suggesting a potential spread of HIV to uninfected prisoners (Murphy, Gaffney, Carey, Dooley & Mulcahy, 1992).

A more recent study of HIV and hepatitis B/C prevalence among prisoners investigated the sharing of injecting equipment in the prison setting (Allwright et al., 1999). As may be expected in an environment where there is no formal access to injecting equipment, it was found that injecting drug users were more likely to share injecting equipment while in prison than when they were in the community. Of injecting drug users, 58 per cent reported that they had shared all injecting equipment (i.e. needles, syringes, filters, spoons) while in prison, compared to 37 per cent who reported sharing in the month prior to being incarcerated. Furthermore, of those injecting drug users who had shared injecting equipment inside the prison, 89.1 per cent had tested positive for hepatitis C.

2.3.2 Sexual Risk Behaviour

In 1985 Irish family planning legislation was amended to allow for the sale of condoms to people over the age of 18 without a prescription from a range of named outlets. The sale of condoms was not deregulated in Ireland until 1993, when the law was changed to make condoms available for sale through outlets other than pharmacies. This change in the law was principally in response to public health concerns in relation to HIV/AIDS, and the law referred to condoms as infection preventers rather than as pregnancy preventers (Prendiville & Smith, 1993). Condoms are sold from a wide range of sources, including vending machines. Furthermore, condoms are distributed freely to groups considered to be at high risk of infection, including injecting drug users. Despite the wide availability of condoms, research carried out among drug users suggests that they continue to engage in sexual risk behaviours which may facilitate the spread of HIV and other infectious diseases.

A study of first-time attenders at the Eastern Regional Health Authority needle exchange programmes from 1990 to 1997 found that only 55 per cent of first-time attenders (n=5,152) reported using a condom during sexual encounters in the previous year (Mullen & Barry, 1998). A study of drug-using women working in prostitution (n=77) (O'Neill & O'Connor, 1999), 83 per cent of whom reported injecting drugs in the previous month, found that while 92 per cent 'always' used condoms with clients for vaginal sex, only 15 per cent 'always' used condoms with their partners for vaginal sex. Furthermore, while none reported 'never' using condoms with clients for vaginal sex, 52 per cent reported that they 'never' used condoms with partners for vaginal sex. There were similar findings in research carried out with a cohort of clients attending a syringe exchange programme (n=1,309). It was found that 25 per cent of those who reported having no regular sexual partner reported 'never' using condoms, whereas 41 per cent of clients who reported having a regular sexual partner (n=865) reported 'never' using condoms. It has been argued that the reluctance to use condoms within long-term or steady sexual relationships can be particularly problematic; this has been argued both in the context of the drug-using population (Cox & Lawless, 2000) and the general population (Mahon, Conlon & Dillon, 1998).

2.3.3 Summary

In summary, this section highlights the extent to which Irish drug users continue to engage in behaviours conducive to the spread of drug-related infectious diseases, both through their injecting drug use and their sexual activity. Despite the expansion of harm-reduction strategies since the early 1990s, Irish drug-users continue to engage in these risk behaviours. The findings of studies carried out in the early 1990s in relation to risk behaviours may be explained by a lack of appropriate service provision and a lack of knowledge among both service providers and users of the risks involved in sharing. However, the more recent study findings show that these patterns of risk behaviour continue to exist despite the presence of appropriate services. Section 2.5 presents the research findings on whether the introduction of harm-reduction strategies have had an impact on drug users' risk behaviours.

2.4 Consequences of Drug-Related Infectious Diseases

The consequences of drug-related infectious diseases have not received significant attention in the Irish literature. This chapter explores the data available on both the health-related consequences and the wider social consequences of drug-related infectious diseases.

2.4.1 Health-Related Consequences

The most obvious consequences of HIV and hepatitis B and C infection are the impact these diseases have on the individual's health. There are no data available on the number of drug users who develop chronic hepatitis C infection or require care for hepatitis B infection. The only data collected on the health consequences of drug-related infectious diseases are those on AIDS-related cases and deaths. Since recording began in 1982 and up until 31 December 1999, there have been 691 AIDS cases reported in Ireland, and 349 AIDS-related deaths (see Table 2.6). In 1999 there were 41 new AIDS-related cases recorded. Intravenous drug users continue to represent one of the main risk categories recorded in this data source. In 1999 intravenous drug users accounted for 39 per cent of new AIDS cases, and 41 per cent of the year's AIDS-related deaths.

Another area of concern is the extent to which HIV/AIDS is passed on from mother to baby. From January 1986 to December 1999, a total of 172 HIV-positive cases were attributed to the category 'children at risk', representing 7.84 per cent of the total HIV-positive cases reported over the period (Department of Health and Children). However, this category does not indicate the route of infection and it is therefore not known to what extent HIV among these children is attributable to maternal injecting drug use. However, the statistics collected on AIDS cases and deaths indicate where a child's infection is attributable to maternal drug use. In total, from 1982 to 1999 fourteen children born to drug users were recorded as AIDS cases; this represents 2 per cent of the total 691 cases recorded up to 31 December 1999. Furthermore, there were eight AIDS-related deaths among children of injecting drug users recorded in the same time period, which accounts for 2.3 per cent of the total 349 deaths recorded up to 31 December 1999.

In summary, little is known about the health-related consequences of drug-related infectious diseases in Ireland. While there have been improvements in treatment procedures, particularly in the area of HIV, coping with the impact of the high prevalence rate of hepatitis C infection will present a particular challenge to service providers.

2.4.2 Social Consequences

The close link between social deprivation and problematic drug use in Ireland has meant that those affected by drug-related infectious diseases are generally from areas characterised by high levels of social deprivation. Individuals who may be considered socially excluded may therefore suffer further exclusion as a result of being affected by a drug-related infectious disease. In this context, it is important that the wider social consequences of drug-related infectious diseases be considered. However, little research has been carried out in this field, either on individuals infected, their families or the community at large.

As part of a wider study on heroin use in Dublin's inner city, McCarthy & McCarthy (1997) surveyed twenty-six opiate users and eighteen families in which there was a drug-using member. Among both groups, drug-related infectious diseases were raised as an issue of concern. A number of respondents reported that they had to cope with either their own or a family member's infection and its effects. Particularly acute were the concerns expressed by individuals in families where another member was HIV positive. Twenty-eight of the respondents from the family cohort reported that they had a family member who was HIV positive or living with AIDS. One mother reported that four of her children had died from AIDS-related illnesses between 1989 and 1995 (McCarthy & McCarthy, 1997: 58). It was also found, however, that none of the respondents who lived with a person who was infected with HIV had availed of any formal support services for themselves in relation to HIV/AIDS issues.

O'Gorman (1999) carried out a qualitative study of the experiences of both people directly infected by HIV and also those whose lives were affected by HIV, i.e. the parents, partners, children and siblings of people who were HIV positive. In total, members of nineteen families participated in the study - twenty-six adults and seven children who had been diagnosed HIV positive, and a further twenty-nine adults and fifty-four children who were affected by HIV/AIDS. This study highlights the complex nature of the problems faced by both those infected with and those affected by HIV/AIDS. The problems identified include the trauma involved in being diagnosed; informing other family members (e.g. partners, children), who may be at risk of infection; caring for a child who is HIV positive, when the parent is also HIV positive; complying with treatment

TABLE 2.6
Ireland 1982-1999. AIDS Cases and Deaths by Risk Category.

Numbers

Risk Category	1982-1992		1993		1994		1995		1996		1997		1998		1999	
	Cases	Deaths	Cases	Deaths	Cases	Deaths	Cases	Deaths	Cases	Deaths	Cases	Deaths	Cases	Deaths	Cases	Deaths
Intravenous Drug Use Related*	142	61	43	21	22	27	25	27	34	17	10	1	12	8	16	7
Homo/Bisexual Haemophiliacs/ Heterosexuals	109	45	13	14	27	11	16	11	34	16	12	3	13	9	13	5
Others	52	27	12	9	18	6	13	8	11	1	8	2	14	4	11	5
Undetermined	5	3	0	0	0	0	1	0	0	0	2	1	2	0	1	0
Total	308	136	68	44	67	44	55	46	79	34	32	7	41	21	41	17

Source: Department of Health and Children / Virus Reference Laboratory.

Includes categories 'intravenous drug users', 'homo-bisexual/intravenous drug users' and 'babies born to intravenous drug users'.

regimes; and coping with an AIDS-related death. O'Gorman (1999) argues that in the absence of adequate public information campaigns, HIV and AIDS continue to be widely viewed within Irish society with 'prejudice, fear and ignorance' (O'Gorman, 1999: 55). Consequently, those infected with the disease and their families have to live with the added strain of coping with the stigma and secrecy that surrounds HIV.

In summary, as in other European countries, the consequences of drug-related diseases in Ireland are multi-faceted. While they encompass consequences on the health and general well-being of the infected individual, they also impact on the infected individual's family and wider community. The wider social consequences of drug-related infectious diseases have been largely neglected in the Irish context and are in need of further attention.

2.5 New Developments and Uptake of Prevention/Harm Reduction and Care

As mentioned in previous sections, harm-reduction strategies play a key role in the provision of services for drug users in Ireland. Both needle exchange programmes and those based on substitution treatment were expanded in an attempt to curb the spread of HIV among injecting drug users. More recently, there has been an increased focus on the role these services play in preventing the spread of other drug-related infectious diseases, i.e. hepatitis B and C. This section gives an overview of the harm-reduction services available to Irish injecting drug users, which aim to prevent the spread of drug-related infectious diseases among this population. Furthermore, the section gives a brief overview of those services that provide care for those already infected. The following areas of service provision will be addressed:

2.5.1 Harm Reduction Programmes
2.5.2 Testing and Treatment
2.5.3 Hepatitis C Vaccination

2.5.1 Harm Reduction Programmes

A number of harm-reduction strategies have been developed, which specifically aim to prevent the spread of HIV and other drug-related infectious diseases among injecting drug users in Ireland. However, the impact of these programmes on infection rates among injecting drug users are unclear. Smyth et al. (1999a) attempted to explore the impact of these programmes on the spread of hepatitis C by carrying out tests for hepatitis C among a cohort of drug users. The cohort included those who had begun their injecting drug use before and after the expansion of harm-reduction programmes in Ireland. Smyth et al. (1999a) argue that the findings suggest that those injecting drug users who began their injecting drug use after the introduction of harm-reduction strategies, demonstrated a reduced risk of hepatitis C infection. However, Smyth et al. (1999a) emphasise that it was not possible to control for other factors that may explain the decline in the hepatitis C infection rate, such as a possible reduction in overall injecting frequency among more recent injectors.

In this section three specific harm reduction services will be briefly overviewed, and any research findings in relation to the impact they may have had on the spread of drug-related infectious diseases presented. The services that will be covered in this section are:

- Information and Education Programmes
- Needle Exchange Programmes
- Substitution Programmes

Information and Education Programmes

Information on drug-related infectious diseases is made available to drug users through a number of sources. Leaflets containing information on what these diseases are and how they are spread are available to drug users from a number of locations, including drug treatment centres, health centres, drop-in centres and voluntary organisations. An information booklet dealing specifically with hepatitis C has recently been produced, which is directly aimed at informing drug users and their families about the disease (Keating, 2000). Furthermore, there have been a limited number of education programmes aimed at informing drug users directly about drug-related infectious diseases and the associated risks. In 1996 the Health Promotion Unit of the Department of Health and Children produced guidelines for effective HIV/AIDS education (Department of Health, 1996). An example of an education programme aimed directly at drug users was established by the Probation and Welfare Service in Mountjoy Prison, Dublin. This Drug Awareness Programme is a four-week programme consisting of one session per week. The principal aim is to educate participants about their drug use and the associated risks. It is aimed at all prisoners with a history of drug use, including those who have ceased their drug use and those who are continuing to use in the prison setting. Included in this programme is a session on HIV and hepatitis.

While education and dissemination of information about drug-related infectious diseases and the associated risks have been an important component in Ireland's prevention strategy, the effectiveness of information dissemination and the impact of such information on risk behaviour is unclear. Prior to the development of the Probation and Welfare Service's Drug Awareness Programme in Mountjoy Prison, an award-winning booklet and video, containing information for prisoners on HIV discrimination, infection and prevention, were produced and were supposedly available to all prisoners. However, a study carried out, based on focus-group interviews with prisoners and former prisoners, found that HIV-positive individuals in the focus groups had seen neither of these materials (O'Brien & Stevens, 1997). Furthermore, as will be discussed in more detail below, Smyth et al. (1999b) found that even where injecting drug users may be attending a treatment service and may have regular contact with health professionals, this does not necessarily result in the drug user developing a better understanding of hepatitis C and the related risk behaviours. Bourke (1998) also found that, in a cohort (n=66) of young injecting heroin users (aged 15 to 22 years) attending services, 'whilst most understood the significance of sharing needles few were aware that sharing barrels, spoons and filters put them at risk' (Bourke, 1998: 4).

It would appear from the evidence available that information is not always passed on to injecting drug users in an effective manner. Despite the existence of education and information materials as part of the prevention strategy in the area of drug-related infectious diseases, it would appear that there is a need for this information and education to be delivered in a more effective manner.

Needle Exchange Programmes

The first needle exchange programme in Ireland was established in 1989. Since then the service has been expanded to include approximately twelve sites. All the sites are located in the Eastern Regional Health Authority (ERHA) area,[5] which includes Dublin City and surrounding areas. Three types of programmes exist:

- The Merchant's Quay Project is a voluntary organisation, which, among other services, provides a needle exchange programme.
- A mobile clinic, which provides low-threshold services to drug users, including a needle exchange and a low dosage methadone programme. This clinic services four areas in Dublin City and the surrounding suburbs on a Monday to Friday basis.
- The remaining programmes are all in statutory services run by the ERHA. These are located in health centres and drug-treatment centres around the city.

A one-for-one exchange of needles is aimed for by all needle exchange services. However, there is flexibility in order to ensure the service is client-friendly. The mean number of needles given out to injecting drug users at first attendance at ERHA exchange programmes is 4.0 (Mullen & Barry, 1998). Overall, the ERHA programmes estimate that approximately 60-70 per cent of needles are returned to its exchange programmes. For 'first-time' clients at the Merchant's Quay Project, the number of syringes and needles given is normally two barrels and six needles (or six microfines) (Cox & Lawless, 2000). In 1998 a total of 16,509 syringes were dispensed by the Merchant's Quay Project through its exchange programme (Cox & Lawless, 2000).

While there has been an expansion in the number of needle exchange programmes available to Irish drug users, a need for further expansion has been identified. An external review of drug services in the Eastern Health Board (EHB) area, has described needle exchange provision in Dublin as 'patchy and not very comprehensive' (Farrell, Gerarda & Marsden, 2000: 13). While it is recognised that community resistance may impact on the expansion of these services, it is argued that there needs to be a wider geographical distribution of these services. Pharmacies have been suggested as a potential source for clean injecting equipment for injecting drug users.

---

[5] Formerly the Eastern Health Board (EHB).

While there are no restrictions on pharmacies in relation to selling injecting equipment in Ireland, anecdotal evidence suggests that, in practice, this rarely happens. Currently there is no central policy or programme under which pharmacists provide needles to injecting drug users. The Pharmaceutical Society of Ireland has stated that it supports 'the principle of needle and syringe exchange. Its members are ready and willing to provide such a service as part of a comprehensive national needle and syringe exchange network' (McDermott, 1999).

In an evaluation of the Merchant's Quay Project's syringe exchange programme, it was found that it had had a positive impact on reducing the incidence of injecting risk behaviours among clients. Clients were questioned about their risk behaviour when they first attended the service and then again after three months. Within this period it was found that there was a 76 per cent reduction in the numbers reporting lending injecting equipment and a 71 per cent reduction in the numbers reporting borrowing injecting equipment (Cox & Lawless, 2000: 69).

Substitution Programmes

Substitution programmes currently account for the majority of treatment programmes available to injecting drug users in Ireland. At the end of August 2000 there were 4,813 clients receiving substitution treatment in Ireland. The service is provided in a range of settings including addiction centres, satellite clinics and from general practitioners in their own surgeries. It is assumed that by providing a substitute opiate (i.e. methadone), and monitoring illicit drug use through urinalysis, participation on a substitution programme will reduce the illicit opiate intake of a client and, in turn, their injecting drug use. However, a secondary function of substitution programmes in relation to preventing the spread of drug-related infectious diseases is the dissemination of information to clients about HIV and hepatitis and associated risk behaviour.

Williams et al. (1990) carried out a study with sixty-nine clients of a methadone maintenance treatment programme to investigate the extent of 'at-risk' behaviour for HIV transmission among those known to be sero-positive, and to measure the degree of positive change in their risk behaviour. It is important to note that this study was carried out in 1988, prior to the introduction of needle exchange programmes by the health board. Of those who were HIV positive (n=48), 63 per cent admitted that they had continued to share injecting equipment since getting a positive test result. However, when comparing their reported pre-test activities, the findings were deemed to be encouraging. Prior to being tested, 98 per cent reported that they had shared injecting equipment, compared to 63 per cent after testing.

More recently, in 1997, Smyth et al. (1999b) carried out a study of knowledge regarding hepatitis C among a sample of injecting drug users (n=84) in a treatment setting in Dublin. Included in the sample were individuals who were on a methadone maintenance programme and those who were on a short-term detoxification programme. The researchers' basic hypothesis was that those injecting drug users with increased contact with medical services would demonstrate better understanding of hepatitis C and associated risk behaviours, i.e. a 'dose-response' type effect. This hypothesis was not confirmed. Seventy-three of the sample recognised the four main infection routes, i.e. injecting drug use, sex, transfusion and vertical. However, only 44 per cent recognised activities with no associated risk, i.e. injecting without sharing, smoking heroin, and kissing. Smyth et al. (1999b) express concern about the finding that substantial minorities believe that there is a risk of exposure even when not sharing injecting paraphernalia. They argue that perceived personal vulnerability to infections such as hepatitis C is likely to be a factor in leading individuals to avoid practising unsafe injecting behaviour. Where this vulnerability is diminished by false beliefs about already having been exposed to infection, when actually engaging in 'safe' practices, then the preparedness to share injecting equipment may well increase.

In summary, while section 2.2 showed that a significant proportion of Irish injecting drug users continue to engage in injecting risk behaviours, it would appear from this section that harm-reduction strategies have had some positive impact on injecting drug users' risk behaviours. While there is a need to improve the delivery of some services, the findings suggest that infection rates would be higher in the absence of the current harm reduction strategies.

2.5.2 Testing and Treatment

Testing
Testing for hepatitis and HIV is offered to all those entering treatment and is encouraged by low-threshold services such as needle exchange programmes. In

these settings clients are given test results and may be offered referral to treatment where appropriate. The actual proportion of injecting drug users who have been tested for either hepatitis or HIV remains unknown. A study of HIV and hepatitis B and C prevalence among the prison population (Allwright et al., 1999) found that of 509 prisoners with a history of injecting drug use, 59.3 per cent reported that they had been tested for hepatitis C, 49.6 per cent for hepatitis B and 65 per cent for HIV. In the Cox & Lawless (2000) study of needle exchange attenders, 49 per cent reported that they had been tested for HIV. It has also been found that young injecting drug users (below the age of 25) are significantly less likely to have been tested for either HIV or hepatitis than the older cohort (Cassin et al., 1998). While the specific nature of these study populations needs to be considered, these figures suggest that a significant proportion of drug users have not been tested for the various drug-related infectious diseases.

Treatment

The provision of treatment for those infected with both HIV and hepatitis C is a key aspect of drug-related infectious diseases. Treatment programmes for both HIV and hepatitis C are available free of charge in Ireland. While it is not essential for drug users to be referred by drug treatment clinics for HIV and hepatitis C treatment, this is the route generally followed.

Highly Active Anti-Retroviral Treatment (HAART) is available free of charge to drug users through referral to genito-urinary medicine (GUM) and infectious-disease clinics in Ireland. There are four clinics that provide HAART, three based in Dublin, the fourth in southern Ireland in Cork. The selection of patients for HAART is based on internationally-recommended medical criteria, and the motivation of the individual to undergo the treatment. A drug user generally has to be stable on a substitution programme before he/she will be accepted on to a HAART programme. This is due to problems of compliance with the treatment regime and concerns about the risks of prescribing HAART to those who are continuing to engage in illicit drug use.

Treatment for hepatitis C is also available to drug users where its provision is deemed appropriate. Guidelines have been developed for selecting suitable candidates for hepatitis C treatment. It is generally agreed among service providers that a potential client should be 'drug stable' (i.e. free from street opiates and injecting drug use) for a minimum of a year prior to starting treatment and that they should not be drinking alcohol (Keating, 2000). As with

HAART, it is argued that an individual needs to be drug stable in order to maximise the chances of compliance with the treatment regime involved for hepatitis C. Therefore, while a person with a history of injecting drug use may access treatment for hepatitis C, an active injecting drug user may not.

2.5.3 Hepatitis B Vaccination

Hepatitis B vaccination is available free of charge to all injecting drug users through the drug services and, where the individual is entitled to free medical care, through their general practitioner. However, anecdotal evidence suggests there is a lack of knowledge among drug users about hepatitis B in general, and about the availability of a vaccination. Furthermore, anecdotal evidence suggests that not all service providers are offering drug users the hepatitis B vaccination. While the total proportion of injecting drug users who are vaccinated against hepatitis B is not known, special studies have found that a relatively low proportion report having received a vaccination. A study of those clients attending the Merchant's Quay Project found that only 19 per cent of clients reported having been vaccinated for hepatitis B (Cox & Lawless, 2000). Furthermore, a study of HIV and hepatitis B and C prevalence among committal prisoners (Long et al., 2000) found that of 175 prisoners with a history of injecting drug use, only 23 per cent (n=41) reported that they had been fully vaccinated for hepatitis B. There is also a need to ensure that drug users who begin a course of the hepatitis B vaccination complete the three injections. In their study of HIV and hepatitis B and C prevalence among the prison population, Allwright et al. (1999) found that while 300 respondents reported that they had been vaccinated against hepatitis B, only 184 had completed the three doses.

2.6 Conclusion

There appears to be on-going evidence that a significant proportion of Irish drug users may be infected with at least one drug-related infectious disease. However, analysis of the situation remains restricted in the absence of comprehensive routine data collection in the field. It would also appear that while harm-reduction programmes have played a role in containing the spread of drug-related infectious diseases to some extent, a significant proportion of Irish injecting drug users are continuing to engage in risky behaviours. It would appear that there is a need for more comprehensive education and information dissemination strategies targeted at drug users, and in particular young injectors. Furthermore, there is a need for a more effective delivery of testing services and, in particular, hepatitis B vaccination to drug users.

2.7 References

Allwright, S., Barry, J., Bradley, F., Long, J. & Thornton, L. (1999). *Hepatitis B, Hepatitis C and HIV in Irish Prisoners: Prevalence and risk.* Dublin: The Stationery Office.

Bourke, M. (1998). Methadone treatment to prevent hepatitis C transmission. *EuroMethwork, 13,* 3-4.

Butler, S. (1991). Drug problems and drug policies in Ireland: A quarter of a century reviewed. *Administration, 39,* (3), 210-233.

Cassin, S., Geoghegan, T. & Cox, G. (1998). Young injectors: A comparative analysis of risk behaviour. *Irish Journal of Medical Science, 167,* (4), 234-237.

Cox, G. & Lawless, M. (2000). *Making Contact: Evaluation of a syringe exchange programme.* Dublin: Merchant's Quay Project.

Department of Health (1993). *Report of the Expert Group on the Establishment of a Protocol for the Prescribing of Methadone.* Dublin: Department of Health.

Department of Health (1996). *Guidelines for Effective HIV/AIDS Education.* Dublin: Department of Health.
Department of Health (1997). *Report of the Methadone Treatment Services Review Group.* Dublin: Department of Health.

Dorman, A., Keenan, E., Schuttler, C., Merry, J. & O'Connor, J. (1997). HIV risk behaviour in Irish intravenous drug users. *Irish Journal of Medicine, 166,* (4), 235-238.

Farrell, M., Gerarda C. & Marsden, J. (2000). *External Review of Drug Services for 'the Eastern Health Board'.* London: National Addiction Centre.

Government Strategy to Prevent Drug Misuse (1991). Dublin: Department of Health.

Johnson, Z., O'Connor, M., Pomeroy, L., Johnson, H., Barry, J., Scully, M. & Fitzpatrick, E. (1994). Prevalence of HIV and associated risk behaviour in attendees at a Dublin needle exchange. *Addiction, 89,* 603-607.

Keating, S. (2000). *Hepatitis C: A guide for drug users and their families.* Dublin: Eastern Health Board.

Long, J., Allwright, S., Barry, J., Reaper-Reynolds, S., Thornton, L. & Bradley, F. (2000). *Hepatitis B, Hepatitis C and HIV in Irish Prisoners, Part II: Prevalence and risk in committal prisoners 1999.* Dublin: The Stationery Office.

McCarthy, D. & McCarthy, P. (1997). *Dealing with the Nightmare: Drug use and intervention strategies in south inner city Dublin.* Dublin: Community Response.

McDermott, D. (1999). *The Practice of Pharmacy Guide: A handbook for pharmacists on law, ethics and practice.* Dublin: The Pharmaceutical Society of Ireland.

Ministerial Task Force to Reduce the Demand for Drugs (1996). *First Report of the Ministerial Task Force on Measures to Reduce the Demand for Drugs.* Dublin: Department of the Taoiseach.

Ministerial Task Force to Reduce the Demand for Drugs (1997). *Second Report of the Ministerial Task Force on Measures to Reduce the Demand for Drugs.* Dublin: Department of the Taoiseach.

Mullen, L. & Barry, J. (1998). *Needle Exchange in the Eastern Health Board Region: An analysis of first attenders 1990-1997.* Dublin: Eastern Health Board.

Murphy, M., Gaffney, K., Carey, O., Dooley, E. & Mulcahy, F. (1992). The impact of HIV disease on an Irish prison population. *International Journal of STD & AIDS, 3,* 426-429.

Mahon, E., Conlon, C. & Dillon, L. (1998). *Women and Crisis Pregnancy.* Dublin: The Stationery Office.

National AIDS Strategy Committee (2000). *AIDS Strategy 2000*. Dublin: The Stationery Office.

O'Brien, O. & Stevens, A. (1997). *A Question of Equivalence: A report on the implementation of international guidelines on HIV/AIDS in prisons in the European Union*. London: Cranstoun Drug Services.

O'Gorman, A. (1998). Illicit drug use in Ireland: An overview of the problem and policy responses. *Journal of Drug Issues, 28,* (1), 155-166.

O'Gorman, A. (1999). *No Room for Complacency: Families, communities and HIV*. Dublin: Cairde.

O'Kelly, F. & Bury, G. (1996). An analysis of the effects of HIV infection in a cohort of intravenous drug users. *Irish Medical Journal, 89,* (3), 112-114.

O'Mahony, P. (1997). *Mountjoy Prisoners: A sociological and criminological profile*. Dublin: The Stationery Office.

O'Neill, M. & O'Connor, A. (1999). *Drug Using Women Working in Prostitution*. Dublin: Eastern Health Board.

Prendiville, W. & Smith, M. (1993). A review of family planning in Ireland. *The British Journal of Family Planning, 19,* 246-247.

Smyth, R., Keenan, E., Dorman, A. & O'Connor, J. (1995). Hepatitis C infection among injecting drug users attending the National Drug Treatment Centre. *Irish Journal of Medical Science, 164,* (6), 267-268.

Smyth, B., Keenan, E. & O'Connor, J. (1998). Bloodborne viral infection in Irish injecting drug users. *Addiction, 93,* (11), 1649-1656.

Smyth, B., Keenan, E., O'Connor, J. (1999a). Evaluation of the impact of Dublin's expanded harm reduction programme on prevalence of hepatitis C among short-term injecting drug users. *Journal of Epidemiology and Community Health, 53,* (7), 434-435.

Smyth, B., McMahon, J., O'Connor, J. & Ryan, J. (1999b). Knowledge regarding hepatitis C among injecting drug users. *Drugs: education, prevention and policy, 6,* (2), 257-264.

Williams, H., Mullan, E., O'Connor, J. & Kinsella, A. (1990). Risk behaviour for HIV transmission in attenders on methadone maintenance. *Irish Journal of Medical Science, 159,* (5), 141-144.

Chapter 3

Cocaine Use In Ireland: An Exploratory Study

Paula Mayock

3.1 Introduction

In Ireland the heroin epidemic of the 1980s, coupled with the public health crisis of HIV transmission through unsafe injecting practices, resulted in a concentration of attention on 'high-risk' drug use categories, most notably heroin and other intravenous drug use. The major focus in the domains of drug policy, treatment and research centred on the 'threats' posed by enduring patterns of drug use, unsafe methods of drug administration and associated risk behaviours. Heroin, being a dominant drug of misuse among individuals receiving treatment, certainly in the greater Dublin area (O'Brien, Moran, Kelleher & Cahill, 2000), has attracted by far the greatest level of interest and attention. This situation is by no means unique to Ireland. As Egginton & Parker (2000) have remarked, 'so distinctive is the impact of this drug that heroin has its own epidemiology' (Egginton & Parker, 2000: 7). In practice, prevalence studies and other empirical research focus on groups, such as opiate users or injectors, who are of concern at a particular time (Frischer & Taylor, 1999). Put differently, attention to particular forms of drug use is very much a function of the drug-political situation in any given jurisdiction (Cohen, 1996).

Despite heroin's prominence, publicity and official concern, the past decade has witnessed increased recognition of the pervasiveness of drug use in society generally. Drug use, traditionally associated with social and economic disadvantage, is increasingly recognised as a widespread social phenomenon and is clearly no longer confined to marginalised communities. School surveys point to a definite increase in the number of young people reporting lifetime use of a range of illicit substances (Grube & Morgan, 1986; Grube & Morgan, 1990;

Hibell et al., 1997; Brinkley, Fitzgerald & Greene, 1999; Hibell et al., 2000). Less is known, in an Irish context, about drug use in the general population as few household surveys, concentrating on adult rather than youth populations, have been conducted. However, a recent population survey, examining the lifestyle, attitudes and nutritional status of people aged 18 to 55 years, revealed a lifetime prevalence rate of 17 per cent for cannabis. Last-year prevalence was estimated at 2 per cent for amphetamines and ecstasy and 1 per cent for tranquillisers and LSD (Friel, NicGabhainn & Kelleher, personal communication). Although cannabis remains by far the most popular of the illicit drugs and the most likely to be used repeatedly across time, available data suggest that other drugs, including amphetamine, ecstasy and LSD, are increasingly likely to be used, particularly by adolescents and young adults. It would appear that we are increasingly living in a drug-conscious society.

In Ireland relatively little attention has focused on the use of individual drugs, with the result that little is known about the extent and nature of specific forms of drug involvement. Attention to drug use, apart from heroin, has concentrated almost exclusively on ecstasy. Reviewing available data pertaining to ecstasy use in Ireland, Bisset (1997) found evidence of an upward trend in use among young people. Murphy, O'Mahony & O'Shea's (1998) comparative research on Irish and European drug policies relating to the use of ecstasy included a small-scale qualitative study of ecstasy use by adults aged between 17 and 27 years. The findings of this research suggest that ecstasy was a component of poly-drug-using careers initiated during the mid- to late-teenage years. Ecstasy use was synonymous with the rave/dance scene and was usually consumed in conjunction with alcohol and other drugs, including amphetamine and/or cannabis. More recently, a larger qualitative study of patterns and levels of ecstasy use in Northern Ireland (McElrath & McEvoy, 2000) found a high proportion of 'heavy users' in their sample of ninety-eight respondents. However, the dosage (i.e. number of tablets) per episode of use varied across the sample and typical reports indicated that many users 'staggered' their intake of ecstasy during individual sessions of use. In common with the findings of Murphy et al. (1998), the concurrent use of ecstasy, alcohol and cannabis was common among users. Although it is not possible, on the basis of current knowledge, to provide a reliable estimate of the prevalence of ecstasy use, the issue has nonetheless been the focus of some research. Other drug use, including amphetamine, LSD and cocaine, have received little or no attention in an Irish context.

The purpose of the current paper is to examine cocaine use in Ireland. This research coincides with renewed attention, in a European context, to suggestions of a possible increase in the availability and use of cocaine. Increases in cocaine use across Europe have been visible since the late 1960s (Erickson, Adlaf, Murray & Smart, 1987). For example, studies in the United Kingdom have shown steady increases in various indicators of cocaine use during the past 10 to 15 years (Marsden, Griffiths, Farrell, Gossop & Strang, 1998; Ramsay & Partridge, 1999). A recent British review of law enforcement figures, treatment statistics and other key prevalence indicators, reveals a steady and significant upsurge in cocaine use from 1991 to 1998, suggesting that the United Kingdom may be witnessing the rapid spread of new cocaine use (Corkery, 2000).

The primary aim of this current research was to investigate levels and patterns of cocaine use in Ireland. The study was undertaken against a backdrop of anecdotal and impressionistic evidence suggesting that cocaine is very much 'around', more easily procured than previously and making a conspicuous breakthrough on the drug scene. Hence, the research sought to locate and analyse all available data identified as potentially useful in an assessment of the extent and nature of cocaine use in Ireland.

The multiple existing data sources used in the research are described in detail below. However, as a starting point, it is helpful to provide a brief overview of the pharmacological properties of cocaine and the principal routes of cocaine administration.

3.2 Pharmacological Dimensions of Cocaine and Modes of Use

Cocaine is a naturally-occurring substance derived from the leaves of the coca plant, *Erythroxylon coca*, a shrub that grows in the Andean area of South America (Fischman & Foltin, 1991). It is an odourless, white crystalline powder and is classified as a central-nervous system stimulant. Cocaine was first extracted in 1855 and later became a popular stimulant and tonic. Up until 1904 Coca-Cola, the popular non-alcoholic beverage, contained small quantities of cocaine (ISDD, 1996).

The most common form of ingesting cocaine is 'snorting' - sniffing fine cocaine crystals via the nostrils. By snorting, cocaine is conveyed into the bloodstream via the mucous membranes of the nose and throat where it dissolves. Cocaine increases feelings of alertness and energy and produces intense euphoria. Negative effects include anxiety, inappropriate levels of aggressiveness, sleeplessness, sweating, impotence and heavy feelings in the limbs. Very heavy users of cocaine may report strong feelings of paranoia.

The smokeable form of cocaine is known as free-base, rock or crack cocaine. The cocaine powder is converted into cocaine base and smoked, usually through a pipe. Crack cocaine is processed with ammonia or sodium bicarbonate (baking soda) and water, and heated to remove the hydrochloride. Because crack is smoked, the user experiences a shorter but more intense high than snorting the drug (Corrigan, 1997; NIDA, 1999). Crack cocaine produces effects far more rapidly than the powder form and this, coupled with the shorter duration of the euphoria, makes crack smoking a potentially highly-addictive substance. However, neither tolerance nor heroin-like withdrawal symptoms occur with repeated use of cocaine (ISDD, 1996). Users may develop a strong psychological dependence on the physical and mental well being afforded by the drug.

Finally, cocaine may be used intravenously, although this mode of ingestion is less common and is viewed as dangerous by most cocaine users (Cohen, 1989). Intravenous injection results in an almost immediate high within fifteen seconds of injecting (Pinger, Payne, Hahn & Hahn, 1995). Some drug users combine cocaine powder or crack with heroin to produce a drug cocktail known as 'speedballs'.

Prolonged heavy cocaine use is usually followed by a 'crash' if use is discontinued. This 'crash' is characterised by exhaustion, restless sleep patterns, insomnia and depression (Erickson et al., 1987). However, there is considerable disagreement over what constitutes 'addiction' or 'dependence' in the case of cocaine. Furthermore, there is little consensus on who is susceptible to or at greater 'risk' of cocaine dependence. Waldorf, Reinarman & Murphy (1991), in a study of 'heavy' cocaine users (users who the authors claim qualify as the most serious 1 per cent of the cocaine-using population), found that even among this group, a large number maintained a stable, although heavy, pattern of use over several years without increasing their cocaine intake. They add that 'it is exceptionally difficult to predict which users will maintain control and which will become compulsive' (Waldorf et al., 1991: 102).

Other research similarly concludes that many heavy cocaine users do not become dependent (Erickson et al., 1987; Cohen, 1989; Chitwood & Morningstar, 1985). Hammersley & Ditton (1994), in a study of Scottish cocaine users not known via their criminality or contact with drug services, conclude that 'cocaine can lead to protracted bouts of heavy or excessive use, but many users can then stop or moderate use prior to encountering problems' (Hammersley & Ditton, 1994: 68).

The accumulated research evidence on cocaine use across several jurisdictions suggests that, among community samples of cocaine users (that is, users not in contact with drug treatment services), even heavy users will not necessarily develop symptoms normally associated with chronic drug dependence. Reinarman, Murphy & Waldorf (1994), summarising three studies of cocaine users (Warldof, Murphy, Reinarman & Joyce, 1977; Murphy, Reinarman & Waldorf, 1989; Waldorf et al., 1991), concluded that addiction is not an inevitable consequence of cocaine's pharmacological action on human physiology. Rather, both cocaine dependence and controlled use of the drug are contingent upon the social circumstances of the user and on the conditions under which cocaine is taken.

On the other hand, Parker & Bottomley's (1996) study of crack cocaine users, many of whom were known to drug services, revealed only a minority of controlled users. Among this group, there appeared to be a complex pattern of dependency on both cocaine and heroin, whereby users were 'psychologically hooked into rock cocaine but physically dependent on heroin' (Parker & Bottomley, 1996: 36). Other research indicates significant differences between treatment and non-treatment cocaine users. Chitwood & Morningstar (1985) found that users in treatment were more likely than community samples to be heavy rather than light users of cocaine, and to be unemployed and lacking in support networks of close friends.

3.3 Research Methodology

There are three research components in this analysis of cocaine use in Ireland. The first (see Section 3.4) examines existing, predominantly statistical, data sources in order to identify emerging patterns and trends in cocaine and base/crack cocaine use. Relevant data from several sources, all considered to be key indicators of drug misuse, are presented. The combined information from the data sources listed below, covering a range of population segments, are presented and analysed.

3.4.1 Law Enforcement and Supply Statistics
3.4.2 Drug Treatment Figures
3.4.3 School-Going, College-Going and General Population Surveys
3.4.4 Morbidity and Mortality
3.4.5 Qualitative and Ethnographic Research

Since no detailed empirical investigations of cocaine use have been undertaken in Ireland to date, two additional components were incorporated into the research in order to generate a more comprehensive picture of current patterns of use and to assess dominant perceptions of the scale of the 'problem'. The emphasis in the first (see Section 3.5) was on accessing 'front-line' indicators, that is, individuals working in the community and at street level who are well-positioned to detect recent or 'new' local developments. This is important since available figures may not accurately reflect current drug trends owing to the time-lag between the collection and the processing and publication of relevant data.

Individual face-to-face and telephone interviews were conducted with a range of informants including drug-service providers, An Garda Síochána, youth workers, drug counsellors, general medical practitioners, hospital personnel, night-club owners and a small number of key informants considered to have experience of and insight into common and preferred drug-taking practices. The primary objective was to access the views, perspectives and concerns of individuals who have direct knowledge and/or experience of cocaine users and of the drug scene generally. In this context, there was a specific focus on uncovering information pertaining to the availability of cocaine, local drug markets, trafficking/dealing/ distribution patterns, health consequences and the negative repercussions of use. In addition, interviews with drug-service staff addressed the issue of service provision, including the needs of cocaine users and implications for treatment intervention and other drug services.

Finally, in view of the widespread recognition of recreational or non-problematic forms of cocaine use in other jurisdictions (Erickson et al., 1987; Cohen 1989; Green et al., 1994; Hammersley & Ditton, 1994), a small-scale qualitative study of adult cocaine users not in contact with drug-treatment agencies was undertaken (see Section 3.6). The primary aim of this exploratory research was to examine respondents' use of cocaine and other drugs. The research also sought to examine attitudes to cocaine and other drug use, to investigate perceptions of the risks associated with cocaine compared to other drugs, and to examine dominant or preferred circumstances associated with the use of cocaine. The selection criteria and recruitment process are discussed in Section 3.6.

In summary, multiple sources were used in order to build a fuller picture from partial data. The orientation of the research is largely investigative, with each segment of data feeding into a 'detective' approach (Douglas, 1976). General principles of analytic induction were applied to the examination of pre-existing data and to data collected through face-to-face and telephone interviews. This approach involved establishing an initial description of the phenomenon and the continued refinement of that analysis in light of further evidence collected in the course of fieldwork. The strength of this method lies in its capacity to consider many alternatives and progress dynamically as opposing or corroborating evidence appears (Adler, 1990). Analytic induction was formulated by Znaniecki (1934), and later refined as a procedure for verifying propositions on qualitative data by Lindensmith (1947) in a study of opiate addiction. It was used by Becker (1963) in his classic study of marijuana users. This research orientation is particularly suited to gathering information in sensitive and 'hidden' areas of human behaviour (Stimson, Fitch, Rhodes & Ball, 1999).

3.4 Existing Data Sources and Other Relevant Empirical Research on Cocaine Use

In this section, the data pertaining to the use of cocaine (and other drugs) from several key data categories are presented. These include law enforcement and supply statistics, purity levels, drug treatment figures, general population surveys, school surveys, cocaine-related deaths, hospital morbidity and other relevant research findings arising from ethnographic and qualitative studies.

3.4.1 Law Enforcement and Supply Statistics

The accuracy of police statistics are a subject of considerable debate (Bottomley & Pease, 1986). One of the main difficulties with law enforcement figures is that they are not contextualised by reference, for example, to specific overt and covert operations or 'luck strikes'. Differences in drug seizures might also reflect variations in drug control strategies across time (Korf, 1992; South, 1995). However, at a local level, drug seizure figures provide a useful broad indicator or sensor of drugs supply and demand (Parker, Bury & Egginton, 1998).

Available statistics pertaining to seizure and offender data are provided in the annual reports of the Garda Síochána (An Garda Síochána, 1990-1998). Table 3.1 presents the figures for seizures of cocaine made by the Gardaí between 1990 and 1999. Seizure figures for heroin, cannabis, MDMA (ecstasy) and LSD are presented for comparative purposes.

TABLE 3.1
Ireland 1990-1999.
Quantities (kg) of Cocaine and Other Drugs Seized by An Garda Síochána.

Year	Cocaine	Heroin	Cannabis Resin	Ecstasy	LSD
1990	1.009	0.578	114.76	N/A	90 u
1991	.031	0.161	1,101.62	429t	3,169 u
1992	9.850	0.794	498.47	271t	13,431u
1993	.348	1.285	4,200.31	744t	5,522 u
1994	.046	4.649	1,460.72	28,671t	16,634 u
1995	21.800	6.400	15,529.00	123,699t	819 u
1996	642.000	10.800	1,933.00	19,244t	5,901 u
1997	11.020	8.211	1,247.88	17,516t	1,851 u
1998	333.167	38.340	2,157.24	604,827t	798 u
1999**	85.554	16.957	2,511.30	229,091t	577 u

Source: Annual Reports of An Garda Síochána, 1990-1999.
Quantities of ecstasy in tabs (t); LSD in units (u).
** 1999 figures are subject to revision as all statistics were not analysed at the time of going to press.
N/A = data not available.

Internationally, it is often estimated that approximately 10 per cent of all drugs in circulation are intercepted (Boekhoutvan Solinge, 1998; Stimson, 1987). Table 3.1 illustrates considerable variation in the quantity of cocaine seized by the Gardaí between 1991 and 1999. A quite dramatic rise in the amounts seized is apparent from 1995. It should be noted, however, that the exceptionally large amounts seized in both 1996 and 1998 make the data susceptible to being skewed (Sutton & Maynard, 1993).

The number of cocaine offences where proceedings commenced between 1990 and 1999 are presented in Table 3.2. The figures for heroin, cannabis and ecstasy are again included for comparative purposes.

TABLE 3.2
Ireland 1990-1999.
Number of Drug Offences by Type of Drug.

Year	Cocaine	Heroin	Cannabis Resin	Ecstasy
1990	11	71	1,413	--
1991	7	45	2,354	45
1992	11	91	2,643	31
1993	15	81	2,895	66
1994	15	230	2,848	261
1995	30	296	2,209	645
1996	42	432	1,441	340
1997	97	564	2,096	475
1998	88	789	1,749	439
1999	169	887	3,281	1,023

Source: Annual Reports of An Garda Síochána, 1990-1999.

The number of individuals charged with, or prosecuted on, a cocaine-related drug offence is small compared to those relating to heroin, cannabis and ecstasy. However, the figures do point to an increase in the number of offences where proceedings commenced between 1990 and 1999. Figures doubled between 1994 and 1995 and increased three-fold again by 1997, with 1999 producing the record figure for cocaine-related drug offences. 'Offender' data do, therefore, suggest that an increase in cocaine possession and supplying is occurring on the ground. However, this same upward trend is evident in relation to heroin, cannabis and ecstasy. Law enforcement strategies need to be considered, therefore, when assessing the quite dramatic increase in the numbers charged or prosecuted on all drug-related offences during the latter half of the 1990s. For example, it may be related to measures taken during this period to extend and strengthen the existing statutory framework for the control of drugs (see Loughran (1999: 328) for a summary of drug-related legislation between 1996 and 1998).

Finally, drug-product data is determined from analyses carried out by the Forensic Science Laboratory of the Department of Justice, Equality and Law Reform. These analyses are conducted on drugs seized by the Gardaí. Information from this source indicates that the purity of cocaine has dropped over the past three years, from 62 per cent in 1996 to 38 per cent in 1998. It should be noted, however, that these figures may not accurately reflect the purity level of cocaine at street level, as no empirical evidence on such a link is available.

3.4.2 Drug Treatment Figures

Unlike heroin, no specific drug is used for the treatment of cocaine dependence and there are no prescription figures that can be used as a proxy measure of cocaine dependence. Hence, data pertaining to individuals receiving treatment for drug-related problems are an important indicator of the level and extent of cocaine use among this group.

The National Drug Treatment Reporting System (NDTRS), operated by the Drug Misuse Research Division (DMRD) of the Health Research Board (HRB), reports data on treatment provided by statutory and voluntary agencies countrywide. It is the primary national source of epidemiological information about drug misuse, providing annual figures on the uptake of services as well as socio-demographic data on clients receiving treatment. The regularity of data collection makes it possible to identify changing patterns and trends in the use of particular drugs across time. Between 1990 and 1994, data were collected in the Greater Dublin area only, but coverage was extended to the whole country in 1995 (O'Brien & Moran, 1997). One of the main advantages of more recent figures pertaining to individuals receiving treatment is that they are regionally sensitive. It should be remembered, however, that the figures relate to those problem drug users who present to services, and not to all those who have a drug problem, or indeed all those who use drugs. The number of cocaine users, even heavy users, outside treatment is likely to be far greater than those who seek treatment (Waldorf et al., 1991).

HRB figures consistently indicate that opiates are the primary drugs of misuse. Four out of five individuals presenting for treatment in Dublin during the period 1990 to1996 reported opiates as their main drug of misuse (O'Brien & Moran, 1997). In 1998, 55.7 per cent of first treatment contacts reported heroin as their primary drug of misuse (O'Brien et al., 2000).

In this section the number of clients reporting cocaine as a drug of misuse in treatment services is examined. It should be pointed out, however, that because the development of drug services in Ireland has been orientated towards problem opiate use, cocaine users may not be attracted to these settings. Table 3,3 illustrates the number of individuals presenting with cocaine as a primary and secondary drug of misuse during the period 1995 to 1998.

TABLE 3.3

Ireland, 1995-1998. Drug Treatment Contacts. Cocaine as Primary and Secondary Drug of Misuse.

Numbers.

Year	Cocaine as Main Drug		Cocaine as Secondary Drug	
	All Contacts	First Contacts	All Contacts	First Contacts
1995	24	10	67	21
1996	25	17	121	50
1997	42	22	195	48
1998	88	32	291	60

Source: National Drug Treatment Reporting System, Health Research Board.

Here we find a clear and consistent increase in the number of all and first-contact clients presenting with cocaine as a drug of misuse during the period 1995-1998. This increase is most dramatic among individuals reporting cocaine as a secondary drug of misuse. The figure for all persons who made contact with drug-treatment services reporting cocaine as a secondary drug of use, shows an increase of over 400 per cent during the period 1995-1998. Individuals presenting with cocaine-related problems were more likely to be male than female. Of the forty-two who reported cocaine as a primary drug of misuse in 1997, thirty-seven were male and five female. The gender breakdown for 1998 is somewhat similar, with seventy-three males and thirteen females reporting cocaine as a main drug. For the year 1998, 72.5 per cent of clients presenting with cocaine as either a primary or secondary drug of misuse were male (O'Brien et al., 2000).

It is important to consider the figures for cocaine misuse in the context of overall drug treatment figures. Taking the 1998 figures as an example, out of a total of 1,625 first contacts nationally, the majority (904 individuals, or 55.7 per cent of the total client group) reported heroin as their primary drug of misuse. This figure was followed by 24.8 per cent reporting cannabis, 7.4 per cent ecstasy, 2.5 per cent methadone, 2.3 per cent amphetamine and 2 per cent reporting cocaine as their main drug of misuse (O'Brien et al., 2000). Hence, individuals reporting cocaine-related drug problems constitute a relatively small proportion of the total number presenting for the first time with drug-related difficulties.

Looking then at the regional breakdown of reported cocaine-related problems among all contacts within each of the health board areas during 1997 and 1998 (see Table 3.4), we find that individuals reporting cocaine as either a primary or secondary drug of misuse are concentrated within particular health board regions.

TABLE 3.4

Ireland 1997-1998. Residents of Health Board Areas Presenting with Cocaine as Primary and Secondary Drug of Misuse within each Health Board Region.

Numbers and Valid Percentages.

Area	All Contacts, 1997				All Contacts, 1998			
	number	%	number	%	number	%	number	%
	Cocaine as Primary Drug		Cocaine as Secondary Drug		Cocaine as Primary Drug		Cocaine as Secondary Drug	
EHB	30	(.7%)	173	(4.2%)	58	(1.1%)	263	(5.2%)
SHB	3	(1.2%)	7	(2.7%)	12	(4%)	7	(2.3%)
NWHB	—	—	—	—	—	—	1	(2.1%)
MHB	—	—	—	—	—	—	1	(1%)
WHB	—	—	—	—	—	—	1	(7.1%)
MWHB	4	(4.0%)	2	(2.0%)	3	(3.1%)	2	(2.1%)
NEHB	2	(2.2%)	4	(4.3%)	2	(1.6%)	1	(0.8%)
SEHB	3	(1.9%)	5	(3.2%)	9	(4.5%)	5	(2.5%)

Source: O'Brien et al., (2000).

The largest number of contacts stating cocaine as a drug of misuse were resident in the Eastern Health Board region. This is hardly surprising given that the majority of treated contacts countrywide occur within this same region. The Southern Health Board and South Eastern Health Board areas had the next highest proportion of treated cocaine contacts in 1997 and 1998.

It is clear from the available figures that greater numbers of individuals than previously are presenting with cocaine-related difficulties. However, cocaine is clearly more likely to be a secondary than a primary drug of misuse. Individuals are less likely to present with cocaine-related difficulties, compared to other drug problems, most notably those related to the use of heroin, benzodiazepines, cannabis and ecstasy.

3.4.3 School-Going, College-Going and General Population Surveys

In Ireland, there is an absence of data, collected at regular intervals, on drug use among the general population and concerning specific groups, including young adults and adolescents. Furthermore, because differing methodologies have been utilised across available surveys, it is difficult to compare drug prevalence rates and establish accurate trends. This section will report on all available data pertaining to cocaine use in school-going, college-going and general populations.

Survey research in Ireland has concentrated primarily on studies of secondary-school students. Grube & Morgan's (1986) study of drug use by 13-16-year-olds in twenty-four randomly-selected schools in the greater Dublin area found a lifetime prevalence rate of 1.5 per cent for cocaine, with 0.7 per cent having used the drug during the month prior to completing the questionnaire. This figure is low compared to 13.2 per cent who had ever used cannabis and 12.9 per cent who reported the use of glue/solvents at some stage in their lifetime. Grube & Morgan's (1990) follow-up study revealed an increase of 0.2 per cent in the numbers reporting past month use of cocaine. Brinkley et al.'s (1999) more recent survey of rates and patterns of substance use among Dublin post-primary pupils did not report on cocaine use.

The most recently-published national study of drug use by adolescents, carried out in 1999 as part of the European Schools Project on Alcohol and Drugs (ESPAD), found that 2 per cent of students aged 15 and 16 years reported lifetime experience of cocaine (Hibell et al., 2000). This figure is identical to that recorded in the 1995 national survey (Hibell et al., 1997). The figures for lifetime use of crack - 3 per cent in 1995 and 2 per cent in 1997 - are surprisingly high, given that reported use of crack is generally considerably lower than that for cocaine among adolescents. For example, the 1998 British Crime Survey revealed that while 3 per cent of 16-19-year-olds reported lifetime use of cocaine, only 1 per cent reported the use of crack (Ramsay & Partridge, 1999).

As with other drugs, including cannabis, ecstasy and amphetamine, regional surveys outside Dublin suggest somewhat lower cocaine prevalence rates than those reported in Dublin samples. A survey of post-primary school students in the Mid-Western Health Board region found that 1.3 per cent reported lifetime use of cocaine and 0.4 per cent were current users of the drug (Gleeson, Kelleher, Houghton, Feeney & Dempsey, 1998). Jackson's (1997) survey of drug use in Cork and Kerry revealed a lifetime prevalence rate of 1 per cent for cocaine. A much smaller proportion (0.1%) reported current use of the drug.

The figures above concur with findings related to school-going populations in the United Kingdom (Barnard, Forsyth & McKeganey, 1996; Balding, 1998) and suggest that cocaine use is relatively rare among adolescents, certainly compared to other drug use. Available figures indicate only a slight increase in the number of Irish adolescents reporting lifetime experience and use of cocaine during the past two decades.

Rather less is known about drug use among college students. A recent survey of drug exposure and alcohol consumption among 366 health service attendees at a Dublin university, revealed cocaine lifetime prevalence rates of 7.1 per cent for males and 4.9 per cent for females. This compared to a lifetime prevalence rate of 50 per cent for cannabis, 16.5 per cent for ecstasy and 10.5 per cent for LSD (Denehan, Clarke & Liossis, submitted).

Few national surveys of drug use prevalence have been undertaken in Ireland. A survey carried out in 1998 by the Health Promotion Unit of the Department of Health and Children and the Centre for Health Promotion Studies, National University of Ireland (NUI), Galway, examined the lifestyle, attitudes and nutritional status of people in Ireland. Cocaine use during the twelve months prior to the completion of the questionnaire was reported by 1 per cent of respondents (Friel, NicGabhainn & Kelleher, personal communication). This is consistent with findings in the United Kingdom, where cocaine use remains at low levels of around 1 per cent or less of adult populations (Baker & Marsden, 1994).

In summary, although surveys suggest that drug use is increasingly a feature of youth culture (Hibell et al., 1997; Brinkley et al., 1999; Hibell et al., 2000), cocaine use remains rare among school-going adolescents and has shown little sign of an increase during the past two decades. Lifetime prevalence among the general population is currently running at approximately 1 per cent.

3.4.4 Morbidity and Mortality

Both morbidity and mortality statistics are of limited value in the estimation of drug use and drug problems in general (Garretsen & Toet, 1992). However, available data relating to morbidity and mortality are presented as an indicator of the extent to which cocaine is implicated in death or illness.

Mortality statistics are based on death certificates, which usually contain information on socio-demographic variables and on the cause(s) of death. Throughout the 1990s there has been a marked increase in the number of drug-related deaths throughout Europe. This upward trend appears to be more pronounced in Ireland than in other European countries (EMCDDA, 1999). The numbers of deaths where drugs were the direct cause of death, during the period 1990-1998, are presented in Table 3.5 and reveal a dramatic increase in drug-related deaths during the 1990s.

TABLE 3.5
Ireland, 1990-1998.
Numbers of Drug-Related Deaths.

Year	All Ages	Age 15-49 Years
1990	7	7
1991	8	7
1992	14	14
1993	18	16
1994	19	19
1995	43	39
1996	53	50
1997	55	52
1998	99	90

Source: Central Statistics Office.

A recent analysis of drug-related deaths investigated by the Dublin City and County Coroners in 1998 and 1999 (Byrne, 2000) reveals that cocaine was implicated in six out of a total of eighty-six opiate-related deaths in 1998 and six cases out of seventy-seven in 1999. Only in one of the 1998 cases, however, was death attributed directly to cocaine overdose, with five of the six cases having two or more drugs implicated in addition to cocaine. Heroin was implicated in all six of the cocaine-related deaths in 1999 and the quantity of heroin revealed in toxicology tests was higher than that for cocaine (Byrne, 2000).

Hospital psychiatric data are available from the National Psychiatric In-Patient Reporting System (NPIRS), which collects data on admissions and discharges from public and private psychiatric hospitals and units countrywide. It provides information on gender, age, marital status, socio-economic status, legal status, diagnosis and length of stay (O'Brien & Moran, 1997). Despite considerable debate about the potential of some illicit substances to cause psychiatric problems, as well as the role of pre-existing psychiatric conditions in the development of drug problems, co-morbidity remains a major concern as elevated levels of drug consumption are found among those with mental health problems (Commission on Narcotic Drugs, 2000). The figures for admissions to psychiatric hospitals with a diagnosis of cocaine use (ICD-10/F14)[1] during the period 1994-1998 are presented in Table 3.6.

TABLE 3.6
Ireland 1994-1998. Psychiatric Hospital Admissions
with Diagnosis of Cocaine Use (ICD 10/F14).

Year	All Ages
1994	18
1995	7
1996	8
1997	5
1998	9

Source: National Psychiatric
In-Patient Reporting System,
Health Research Board.

[1] As defined by The ICD-10 Classification of Mental and Behavioural Disorders: Clinical descriptions and diagnostic guidelines, of the World Health Organisation (1992).

The Hospital In-Patient Enquiry (HIPE) Scheme, operated by the Economic and Social Research Institute, is a system designed to collect medical and administrative data regarding discharges from acute hospitals. Information from private hospitals is not included in this database. One difficulty with these data is that each HIPE discharge represents one episode of care. As a result, double-counting may occur where patients have been admitted to hospital on more than one occasion with the same or different diagnoses. Consequently, these records provide a better indicator of hospital activity than of the incidence of disease. Data relating to principal and secondary diagnoses of cocaine-related discharges are provided in Table 3.7 below.

TABLE 3.7
Ireland 1994-1998. HIPE Figures for Hospital Discharges with Principal and Secondary Cocaine-Related Diagnoses.
Numbers.

	1994	1995	1996	1997	1998
Cocaine Dependence (ICD 304.2)	2	9	11	11	13
Non-Dependent Drug Abuse (Cocaine) (ICD 305.6)	5	20	9	11	19
Accidental Poisoning (Cocaine) (E855.2)	0	5	4	10	4

Source: Hospital In-Patient Enquiry System, Economic and Social Research Institute.

The figures recorded for the diagnosis of cocaine dependence (ICD 304.2) have remained relatively stable during the period 1995-1998. Those for non-dependent drug abuse (cocaine), on the other hand, have tended to rise slightly in recent years, albeit from a low base.

Accepting that mortality and morbidity data are not reliable tools for estimating drug use or drug problems, they can, in association with other data sources, help to improve the interpretation of available information. Cocaine is implicated in relatively few deaths, certainly when compared to heroin. Admissions to psychiatric hospitals with a diagnosis of cocaine use indicate no clear upward trend since 1994.

3.4.5 Qualitative and Ethnographic Research

Qualitative methodologies are particularly suited to accessing 'hidden' drug scenes (Wiebel, 1990). An additional advantage of qualitative research in the drugs research field is that it provides detailed knowledge about types and levels of drug involvement as well as important details pertaining to the lifestyles, attitudes and motives of drug users. However, only a small number of such studies have been conducted in an Irish context. Mayock (2000) investigated drug use and non-use among a sample of fifty-seven young people, aged between 15 and 19 years, including abstainers, drugtakers and problem drugtakers, in an inner-city Dublin community. In this study, very few of the young people described as drugtakers (drug users who did not consider their drug use to be problematic) reported the use of cocaine at any time, and of those who did (n=2), it was generally a one-time experience. Cocaine use was far more prevalent among problem drugtakers (young people who considered their drug use to be problematic). All of the young people in this 'problem drugtaker' category (n=18) reported heroin as their primary drug of misuse. The vast majority (n=14) also reported lifetime use of cocaine and nearly 20 per cent reported cocaine use during the week prior to interview. In general, cocaine use occurred subsequent to heroin initiation and was frequently used in conjunction with heroin and other drugs (mainly benzodiazepines). Most users of the drug reported the intravenous use of heroin and cocaine, a drug cocktail known as 'speedballs'. The reports below provide some insight into the nature of this group's cocaine involvement.

Interviewer: *When did you start using cocaine?*

Respondent: *Am, there was a big drought on and everyone was just, there was no heroin, so everyone was taking coke. I was taking tablets like for me sickness, I was going round stupefied on tablets, d'ya know what I mean, and then the coke just ... everyone just got strung out on coke.*

(Female, 18.1 years)

Interviewer: *Did you use coke when you were on gear?*

Respondent: *Yeah, used to mix it. Used to wash up the coke into the drugs, like cook the gear into the works, bung the two of them into me together. Then I would be gettin' a buzz like off the coke and then when I'm coming down off the coke the gear would bring me down nice.*

(Male, 19.1 years)

Finally, McElrath & McEvoy's (2000) qualitative study of ecstasy users in Northern Ireland revealed that 43 per cent of respondents had tried cocaine powder. The mean age of the sample (n=106) was 25 years (range 17 to 45 years). Cocaine use appeared to be sporadic, not regular, and only one respondent reported snorting cocaine on a monthly basis during the six months prior to the interview. This finding suggests that cocaine was one of numerous drugs tried or used by this group of young recreational poly-drug users.

3.4.6 Conclusion

The question of how many people are using illicit drugs is notoriously difficult to answer. The dearth of regular prevalence studies at both national and local levels, using uniform or comparable methodologies, compounds this problem. However, the difficulties associated with establishing accurate and reliable drug-use prevalence estimates is not just about the absence or paucity of relevant survey data. The illegality of drug use ensures that the activity is undertaken inconspicuously and that many drug users remain hidden. The best way, in the present situation, to assess the extent of particular forms of drug use is to utilise all available data from a wide range of sources (Choquet & Ledoux, 1990; Hay, 1998).

Accepting that available sources such as survey and other empirical data can produce, at best, imperfect approximations, there are a number of conclusions that can be drawn from the data presented above. First, there is some evidence to suggest an increase in the supply of and demand for cocaine. Extensive use of the drug, however, is not apparent among the general population. While there is a general upward trend in drug experimentation among school-going teenagers, cocaine is far less likely to be used than cannabis, ecstasy, LSD and amphetamine. Among adult population samples, use appears to be restricted to a minority. The difficulty with these findings, however, is that they fail to uncover substantial knowledge about individuals who do use cocaine.

At the other end of the drugs spectrum are individuals who develop drug problems. Many, though not all, are known to drug treatment services. While heroin remains the primary drug of misuse among drug users who seek treatment, available figures suggest that cocaine is currently more likely to be cited as a secondary drug of misuse. Irish drug treatment data indicate that cocaine is rarely clients' primary problem. Yet, there is evidence to suggest that the drug repertoires of long-term 'problem' drug users have extended to include a larger and more diverse range of substances including, among others, benzodiazepines and cocaine (Farrell, Gerada & Marsden, 2000; Rooney, Kelly, Bamford, Sloan & O'Connor, 1999). However, while cocaine is clearly available and increasingly likely to be used, it is clearly less endemic, certainly compared to heroin, benzodiazepines, cannabis and ecstasy.

3.5 Views of Service Providers and Key Informants on the Cocaine 'Problem'

As stated earlier, this component of the research was concerned with accessing current perceptions of the extent and nature of the cocaine 'problem', from the perspectives of individuals working, or in regular contact, with drug users. The value of this data relates to its potential to report on current and 'new' developments on the ground. Tables 3.8 and 3.9 provide a breakdown of the number and range of individuals interviewed face-to-face and by telephone.

<table>
<tr><td colspan="2">TABLE 3.8
Face-to-Face Interviews</td><td colspan="2">TABLE 3.9
Telephone Interviews</td></tr>
<tr><th>Individual Interviews</th><th>Number of Interviews</th><th>Telephone Interviews</th><th>Number of Interviews</th></tr>
<tr><td>Drug Service Staff</td><td>5</td><td>Student Welfare Service</td><td>2</td></tr>
<tr><td>Youth Worker</td><td>1</td><td>Youth Workers</td><td>2</td></tr>
<tr><td>Youth Work Co-Ordinator</td><td>1</td><td>Project Worker s (Young People)</td><td>2</td></tr>
<tr><td>Key Informants</td><td>2</td><td>Drug Service Staff</td><td>2</td></tr>
<tr><td>Garda</td><td>1</td><td>Liaison Midwife</td><td>1</td></tr>
<tr><td>Night-Club Owner</td><td>1</td><td>General Practitioners</td><td>3</td></tr>
<tr><td>Hospital Personnel</td><td>1</td><td>Garda</td><td>1</td></tr>
<tr><td>Drug Counsellors</td><td>2</td><td>Hospital Personnel</td><td>1</td></tr>
<tr><td>General Practitioner</td><td>1</td><td>Prison Staff</td><td>1</td></tr>
<tr><td>Total</td><td>15</td><td>Total</td><td>15</td></tr>
</table>

Efforts were made to incorporate a cross-section of respondents, in terms of the nature of their experience of drug users and the drug scene. Table 3.10 summarises the issues addressed in the case of each 'subgroup' of interviewee. Separate interview schedules were designed for the respective 'subgroups' of study respondents where appropriate.

TABLE 3.10.
Issues Addressed During Face-to-Face and Telephone Interviews.

Interviewees	Issues Addressed
Drug Service Staff	Numbers presenting with cocaine-related difficulties (stable, increase, decrease) / Evidence of crack cocaine? / Cocaine as a primary drug of misuse? / Treatment needs of cocaine users / Implications for treatment and service provision.
Key Informants*	Who is using cocaine (age group/background/SES)? / Availability, cost and purity? / Is cocaine more accessible than previously? / In what kinds of settings is use taking place? / Patterns of use (regular/recreational/occasional etc.)?
Gardaí	Drug seizures and arrests: have the figures for cocaine changed dramatically in recent years? / Any indicators of increased availability of cocaine at street-level? / If yes, how have the Gardaí responded to this 'new' development?
Youth Workers (within 'high risk' localities)	Is there evidence of increased use of cocaine among young people? / Any evidence to suggest that cocaine is easier to access and/or more affordable than previously? / What are the dominant perceptions of the 'risks' associated with cocaine use? / Are youth workers adequately equipped to respond to current drug use trends?
Night-Club Owners	Which drugs are most visible/available on the club/dance scene? / Any evidence of cocaine use? / If so, when did this come to your attention? / Is cocaine more easily available than previously? / Cost and accessibility?
General Practitioners	Numbers presenting with cocaine-related difficulties (stable, increase, decrease) / Evidence of crack cocaine/ cocaine as a primary drug of misuse / Treatment needs of cocaine users / Implications for treatment and service provision.
Hospital Personnel	Any evidence of cocaine emerging as a drug of choice? / Accident and emergency admissions?

* Key informants are individuals who have experience of and contact with the drug scene and are considered to have knowledge and insights that may contribute significantly to the data collected from other sources.

Interviewing took place during May 2000. Face-to-face interviews were tape-recorded and partial transcripts of this material prepared. Detailed notes were taken both during and after telephone interviews. The major issues and themes arising from these data are documented in this section. The presentation of findings concentrates on the key questions outlined in Table 3.10 and on other issues raised by informants in the interviews. For the purpose of clarity and structure, the findings are presented under three broad headings: cocaine availability, the extent and nature of cocaine use and implications for drug treatment and service provision.

3.5.1 Cocaine Availability

The majority of respondents believed that cocaine was more easily available than previously. Across the range of individuals interviewed, there was a definite consensus on increased accessibility and use of the drug. A spokesperson from the Garda National Drug Unit described the current situation vis-à-vis cocaine availability in the following terms.

> We are quite aware that cocaine is being used and offered for sale, particularly in certain areas. If we look at the statistics in relation to cocaine for say 1998, that shows quite an amount of cocaine being seized. We have 333 kilos and 167 grams. This is a huge amount. Now some of that of course, came from major seizures. But, coke has become more popular. I would have no hesitation saying yes, it is more prevalent.
>
> (Garda)

Several respondents involved in the delivery of drug treatment stated that they had become aware of an increase in the supply of cocaine within the areas where they worked, particularly during the past year.

> You hear about it more and it's almost becoming a substitute drug for heroin. With the availability of methadone now people's need for heroin isn't so great.
>
> (Drug Counsellor)

Similarly, many professionals working with young people in communities where drug use is concentrated drew attention to a shift in the local drugs market towards increased cocaine availability.

> There is a strong sense that it's out there alright. I've no concrete evidence from the group we work with but a very strong sense that it's out there and available.
>
> (Youth Work Co-Ordinator)

My impression is that during the past year or year-and-a-half there has been a lot of selling going on and a good bit of use. Yeah, it's definitely amongst problem drug users and I think that you'd probably find a good number of urines testing positive for cocaine.

(Youth Worker)

Other respondents highlighted the apparent decrease in the street price of cocaine and felt that this served as a further indicator of the changed nature of availability and use of the drug.

It would seem now at the moment that a half a gram can be as low as £25. A number of years ago it was £300 a gram. Now it is down to between £60 and £80 a gram. One thing that is noticeable is that the price varies depending on where you buy.

(Drugs Worker)

It is also significant that a number of individuals involved in the provision of methadone treatment reported a conspicuous upsurge in the proportion of urine samples revealing quantities of cocaine during the latter months of 1999 and the early months of 2000. Although this trend appears to have since abated, doubt was expressed, in some cases, about the validity of the assumption that a decrease in the percentage of urines revealing cocaine can be reliably viewed as an indicator of a downward trend in cocaine use among clients receiving treatment.

The prevalence rate (of cocaine in urines) would appear to be running at around 3 per cent of the known drug users, the ones in treatment. Again, I think that's probably coloured by the fact that cocaine is short-lived in the system. Drug users can very easily get around the system and continue to use cocaine. If say, somebody is clear of every other drug and they're on weekly take-outs it's not a big deal for them to make sure that they don't use two days before they come in to pick up their methadone. So how much of an indicator it is I don't know. There certainly was a peak in the three months of December, January and February but that seems to have gone down again. Now whether it is that it's been challenged and drug users are altering their behaviour or whether they've just managed to work the system, I don't know.

(Drugs Worker)

It is important to state that the perceived increase in cocaine availability and use was associated with particular geographical locations in the Dublin area, which, in the absence of more definitive evidence, will remain unidentified in this paper.

However, the most likely localities to be mentioned included two specific areas associated with concentrations of known drug users. A range of respondents, including drug service providers, general practitioners and the Gardaí, drew attention to particular 'pockets' of high cocaine availability.

From the point of view of gaining insight into individuals in the community who do not identify themselves as drug users per se, interviews were conducted with a number of key informants with knowledge of, and/or contact with, the recreational drug scene. These respondents indicated that cocaine was currently more visible on the club/dance/drug scene than previously. It was also suggested that this trend was accompanied by increased acceptance of cocaine as a drug of choice.

> *I'm not into cocaine myself and I don't really hang out with people who are, ya know, but I know of people who are. I know it's become a usual thing for lots of people. It's just a natural normal thing that they do. There's definitely some people who get more into it and prefer to do coke and there's also that thing where it's seen as a slightly, you know, more prestigious. Coke has always been seen as a middle class drug; for people who have money essentially. You can link it directly in this country to the economic situation. People have more money, they're more affluent and cocaine is a more affluent drug.*

(Key Informant # 1)

The majority of respondents stated that there was little evidence to suggest that crack cocaine was making a breakthrough on the drug scene. However, one interview with an ex-cocaine dealer and former crack cocaine addict suggested some use of 'home-made' crack cocaine among particular networks of drug users. This respondent described himself as 'in recovery' at the time of interview, having previously had a chronic cocaine and heroin problem. He stated that he had been involved in the distribution of cocaine, both within and outside of the Dublin area, for several years.

> *I went as far as South Dublin and out of Dublin to deal. I would travel, yeah. And people would travel from everywhere ta me or else, if they couldn't make it I'd make me way out ta them. Inner-city, apartments as well, ya know, well-ta-do people ... everywhere ... this would be sellin' cocaine. On most occasions I would have ta wash it up for them, turn it into crack for them like. Very few would actually just, very few people I actually dealt with were buying it ta snort, they were buying crack.*
> *[But people say that there's no crack around?]*

I hear this, and I've said it to [name of friend], and it actually makes me blood boil 'cos there's a big problem out there like and it's like, look at heroin in the 80s. It was actually around before then but no, it's nothing, it's only a handful of people, that's what they said. And look at it now! And there's as much coke out there now as heroin. It's so easy to get, ya know.

(Key Informant # 2)

Overall, the data points to increased awareness of the presence of cocaine, its availability on the street, and its potential to become a drug of choice for both recreational and problematic drug users.

3.5.2 Nature and Extent of Cocaine Use

The identification of drug use patterns at local level is difficult to quantify and requires specialist research (Parker et al., 1998). Hence, the aim here is not to advance evidence on the extent of cocaine use generally or among particular sub-groups of the population. Rather, the emphasis is on documenting perceptions of what is occurring on the ground, based on the reports of individuals who have regular contact with drug users.

A conspicuous feature of informants' reports was that despite the general belief concerning increased cocaine availability, many simultaneously felt that they had no concrete evidence of cocaine's emergence as a major issue, certainly compared to heroin and other drug use. In particular, respondents felt unable to estimate the extent of cocaine use in the communities where they worked. There appeared to be a number of important factors associated with this absence of clear evidence or knowledge of cocaine's 'position' or status as a drug of use. First, respondents felt that cocaine use was extremely hidden and consequently, unlikely to come to their attention. Secondly, according to a large number of interviewees, cocaine users are unlikely to perceive their drug use as problematic and accordingly, are unlikely to seek treatment or advice of any kind in relation to their cocaine consumption.

I'm not sure that this area is awash with cocaine but what I would have a sense of is that the ones who are using cocaine are not in touch with services because they don't really see themselves as having a problem.

(Drugs Worker)

You see, young people wouldn't seek treatment around that. Young people do come forward for treatment but it's mostly for heroin. They wouldn't see their use of cocaine as something they can get help for, or that they need help for.

(Youth Worker)

The picture that I'm getting is that the young people who start using coke don't see themselves as having a drug problem because they're not on heroin. So, heroin is still the biggie in people's perceptions and by taking coke you're avoiding having a drug problem.

(Drug Counsellor)

However, a number of professionals working in the delivery of drug treatment at community-level did report direct experience and evidence of cocaine use and considered this development to be a recent one. All stated that users were far more likely to be smoking or injecting cocaine than using the drug intranasally.

Although most of the people who access this service have an opiate problem, I have had contact with cocaine users. One person I'm thinking of now started using on holidays overseas and later developed a dependency.

(Drug Counsellor)

I think it (cocaine) is a serious problem, it's been a serious problem for quite a while. There's a lot of it going around in the flats. And we have an ongoing struggle with people on treatment who might be doing fairly okay as regards the heroin but dabbling or more than dabbling with cocaine.

(Drug Service Coordinator)

Two respondents made specific reference to cocaine use among women. This is particularly noteworthy in view of the findings of a recent study of drug-using women working in prostitution in Dublin city (O'Neill & O'Connor, 1999). Of the seventy-seven women interviewed for the purpose of the research, forty reported use of cocaine in the previous month. Following heroin and benzodiazepines, cocaine emerged as the next likely drug to be used.

Most of the clients who report cocaine use to me are women. And all of them say that it's very difficult to get off the drug, more difficult than heroin. These women would also be working on the street and there seems to be a link between the two.

(Drug Counsellor)

Despite several examples of reports of cocaine use by clients, the dominant concern among respondents involved in the delivery of drug treatment remains firmly on problems related to heroin use. There was general agreement, however, that cocaine was far more likely than previously to be a secondary drug of misuse. Many respondents made reference to the practice of 'speedballing', which involves the simultaneous intravenous use of cocaine and heroin. This practice was described by one of the study's key informants (a former heroin addict) in the following terms:

> What I did then was I made speedballs. Ya know what a speedball is? Ya put your heroin on the spoon and cook it up, have your coke in the works, ya suck it up. The effects ya get from that! You're straight up in the air, like your head feels like it's goin' to go 'bump'. It's a great feelin'! And then ya sorta come down then nice and easy. It's the sorta feelin' (pause), it's unbelievable. It'd frighten ya at first 'cos ya think you'll die but this feelin' ya get from it it's, ya know, it takes all the pain away and all this shit, that's what it's there for at the end of the day.
>
> (Key Informant # 2)

Several respondents acknowledged that 'speedballing' was a common practice and a number drew attention to the health implications of injecting risk behaviour.

> What we would find here is that most people are speedballing, they're using a combination of heroin and cocaine together. So, in terms of harm reduction and looking at issues around health, the same difficulties will arise if people are using needles and injecting cocaine.
>
> (Drugs Worker)

Furthermore, respondents consistently drew attention to dominant risk perceptions and felt that drug users were unlikely to perceive cocaine use as posing serious health risks, certainly compared to those associated with heroin. There is an implicit danger here, if, as perceived, cocaine is increasingly gaining acceptance and is more commonly in use.

> I think the preference here [at the service] among drug users has been for the type of effects that heroin gives. Cocaine would not be seen by most of them as abuse. It would be seen as recreational. They don't see it as such a problem.
>
> (Drugs Worker)

Heroin, as I said before, has that dirty, filthy, low-life thing and all of that, even though it hits all walks of life. Cocaine is looked at, 'ah, it's alright, it's only a line a coke'

(Key Informant)

I think that the dominant perception is that cocaine is primarily a recreational drug, just as hash is understood as a recreational drug. The effects aren't as dramatic or rapid. And this is a problem too because I would certainly meet people who have serious problems with cocaine.

(Drug Counsellor)

It is important to point out that not all of the respondents reported concern about cocaine use among their client group. This is important since it suggests that particular settings and services may be more likely than others to attract cocaine users. A number of respondents stressed that opiates and benzodiazepines remained their overwhelming concern.

We have heroin problems and all sorts of other problems, tablets and all that. But from my point of view, and this is just an overview, we don't get cocaine coming up as a major issue. And it seems to me that there's a couple of angles on that, if we generally accept that heroin is the drug of choice. People will dabble with cocaine, but that's it, they'll dabble but they'll revert to heroin. So, cocaine might be cheap on the streets, they might go for that for a while, it may become problematic with them but they quickly get out of it and back almost to the safety of heroin, the known substance, the known area like.

(Drugs Worker)

Finally, while concern was expressed by the majority of respondents about an apparent increase in the availability and use of cocaine, the problem was not considered to have reached epidemic proportions, as yet, or to merit being perceived as 'out of control'. One informant, who previously worked with cocaine and crack cocaine users in London, drew a clear line of distinction between the situation in Dublin and that which prevailed in London a number of years ago, particularly in terms of service needs and responses.

A serious crack problem developed and all of a sudden agencies were inundated with these people and nobody could relate to them. And we had to do a lot of training to adjust to dealing with these people because it was totally different. The way you'd approach a heroin user, you wouldn't approach a crack user like that. But we're not getting that here. (Drugs Worker)

To summarise, cocaine use was judged to be far more widespread than previously. However, respondents found it difficult to estimate the scale or extent of use among their client groups, or in the community at large. While the majority felt that the cocaine 'problem' was not comparable to that relating to heroin, they identified cocaine use as an issue requiring attention also.

3.5.3 Implications for Drug Treatment and Service Provision

Interviewees engaged in the provision of services to drug users were asked whether the needs of cocaine users can be adequately met within the context of existing treatment interventions. Considerable variation emerged among this group on the appropriate way to address cocaine use in the context of existing services. While some respondents felt that specific tailor-made interventions were required to deal with the needs of cocaine users, others believed that current services needed to develop the knowledge and expertise required to deliver appropriate intervention and counselling. Some respondents stated that their agencies had already attempted to address the issue informally.

> *I would say that there is a need for separate interventions. It's a separate drug, a separate addiction, one which can't be treated like heroin. If the two drugs are lumped in together, then it follows that they're going to be used together. If cocaine users are in a methadone clinic they're bound to pick up the habits that are all around them.*
>
> (Drugs Worker)

> *I do think it's a different kind of problem and one of the reasons it's different is that there doesn't seem to be the same physical withdrawal difficulties but there is an enormous psychological withdrawal and psychological cravings. So what we've done here is supported the person as best we could, get them into counselling and we would also have treated them with acupuncture.*
>
> (Project Worker)

> *I think that as an agency we've already started to change our approach, even in thinking what services can offer somebody who might have a dependency on cocaine. There's no medical treatment so we have been looking at some level, looking at ways that we can provide appropriately as a service.*
>
> (Drug Counsellor)

More critical perhaps than the lack of agreement on appropriate interventions was the fact that several interviewees involved in drug treatment delivery felt ill-informed and ill-equipped to deal with the presenting behaviours and problems of cocaine users. In addition, a number of respondents drew attention to the absence of information on cocaine use and related risk behaviours at community level.

> *They've [drug users] had more information, more education on heroin so maybe they haven't had enough information about cocaine. Initially, they don't have a fear of cocaine because they would believe that it isn't addictive.*
>
> (Drug Service Co-ordinator)

Prevailing perceptions of the risks associated with cocaine use were considered to be a compounding factor. One informant stressed the importance of contextualising current perceptions of drug-related risk when attempting to alter behaviour and beliefs about cocaine.

> *It's largely a methadone culture and that's the context I'm speaking in. And methadone is perceived as the solution to the problem. And for people who are seriously dependent on cocaine and want help, the belief is that methadone is the solution for them as well and therefore, they want methadone treatment. That's the perception in the community. So we would have had to be quite strong in helping people to understand that it's a totally different drug and that there's absolutely no point putting the person on methadone, that you're actually introducing them to opiates. But this is all understandable in the context of a strong heroin and methadone culture.*
>
> (Drugs Worker)

Most respondents agreed that there was a need for more information and training on the effects of cocaine, the presenting behaviours of cocaine users and appropriate treatment and intervention options.

3.5.4 Conclusion

Using existing data systems, including available data on drug users, Section 3.4 found that opiates remain the primary drugs of misuse among drug users who access treatment. Despite this, subtle indicators of a shift in the drugs landscape were apparent, suggesting increased likelihood of cocaine use among individuals whose main drug of misuse was heroin. The reports of drugs workers confirm this trend. A large number stated that clients are now more likely to present with cocaine-related problems and the majority felt strongly that cocaine was more readily available and accessible than previously. The risk of 'microdiffusion', that is, the dispersal of drugs knowledge, practices and techniques through established user networks (Parker et al., 1998), may be substantial if, as indicated, cocaine is making a breakthrough on the drug scene. Further research is required to qualify and quantify a possible spread of cocaine use among problem drug users. In particular, the nature of the relationship between heroin and cocaine, one known to be complex (Bottomley, Carnwath, Jeacock, Wibberley & Smith, 1997), requires investigation. Qualitative research is likely to be the most feasible means of accessing these 'heavy-end' and hidden drug scenes (Brian, Parker & Bottomley, 1998a). Preferred routes of cocaine administration and related risk behaviours need particular attention in this context. Blanken & Barendregt (1997) note that the Dutch cocaine smoking epidemic was restricted mainly to heroin-dependent persons. Furthermore, Grund, Adriaans & Kaplan's (1991) investigation of cocaine use in a sample of heroin addicts in Rotterdam found that the mode of ingestion paralleled that of heroin: injecting drug users injected cocaine-hydrochloride and heroin smokers smoked cocaine base. The authors documented the distribution of 'gekookte coke', otherwise known as 'cooked', 'base' or 'rock' cocaine, by a particular sub-population of drug users. The preparatory process is identical to that described by one of the current study's key informants, a former user and supplier of 'homemade' crack cocaine.

> *Well, basically all ya do is (pause) ya can add ammonia. That's a lazy way ta do it. I call it the lazy man's way a doin' it. Ya put your coke on the spoon, your gram a coke or whatever ya have on the spoon, ya pour a dribble of ammonia over it, light a flame underneath it. It's like cookin' heroin. It bubbles like fuck and it goes inta sort of an oil and ya leave it cool or else ya can drain it off. Ya rinse it with cold water then, ya don't heat it up again, ya just rinse it with water 'cos if ya do that it'll just dissolve inta ... And then ya take it off. And ya know a hash pipe? Like a seven-up bottle or something. Instead of using tobacco ya use the ash off the cigarette. It has ta be fresh ash. So like you'd have one ashtray for cigarettes, for puttin' out your cigarette. You'd have cigarettes burning everywhere but ya wouldn't put the cork out on it 'cos ya want the ash. Ya just break bits a lump off it and whatever and (inhales) ya smoke it and ya get your couple a seconds hit.*

(Key Informant # 2)

At present, there is no way of establishing either how widespread the practice of 'cooking' (or 'rocking') cocaine is, or how prevalent this technique is among drug users. However, problem opiate users are far more likely to be injecting or smoking than to be snorting cocaine (Grund, Adriaans & Kaplan, 1991).

Research is required to explore dominant and preferred patterns of cocaine use among both treatment and community samples of heroin users. Brian et al.'s (1998a) follow-up investigation of continuity and change in crack cocaine users' drug careers in north-west England found that, owing to crack's negative image, dealers sold it as 'rock' or 'stone', particularly to new, younger users. Knowledge about the marketing of cocaine, including users' accounts of initial points of contact with the drug, and acquired (or recommended) techniques of use, would greatly assist targeted strategies, including advice on harm minimisation, particularly to 'high-risk' young drug users.

Finally, the treatment needs of individuals who co-abuse opiates and other substances require attention. Rooney et al. (1999), comparing Irish drug users who are dependent on opiates and benzodiazepines with drug users who are not dependent on benzodiazepines, found that the former group tended to take more drugs in general. Thirty-five per cent of those dependent on opiates and benzodiazepines used cocaine, compared to 13.8 per cent of the opiate users not dependent on benzodiazepines. More recently, Farrell et al. (2000) analysed the results of urine tests for opiates, benzodiazepines and tricyclics carried out in five addiction clinics across the Eastern Health Board area and found that 65 per cent tested positive for benzodiazepines. The authors conclude that this high rate of positivity indicates 'a major problem of poly drug misuse which requires urgent and concerted attention' (Farrell et al., 2000: 8). Further confirmation of extensive poly-drug use among heroin users can be found in Byrne's (2001) analysis of 254 opiate-related deaths investigated by the Dublin City and County Coroners in 1998, 1999 and 2000. This research identified poly-drug use as a major risk factor associated with fatal drug overdose. A single drug was implicated in only a minority (6.7%) of fatalities, with heroin implicated in 61.8 per cent, benzodiazepines in 70.5 per cent, methadone in 56.7 per cent and cocaine in 6 per cent of cases.

Despite considerable evidence indicating poly-drug use, including cocaine use, among individuals who seek treatment for heroin-related problems, relatively little is known about the nature of combination or poly-drug-using careers. This represents a significant gap in knowledge, given the likely range of treatment challenges arising from the current tendency, across Europe, for heroin users to become poly-drug users (Brian, Parker & Bottomley, 1998b). Bottomley et al. (1997) note that, in general, research has provided little guidance as to how drug services can help problematic cocaine users, or, for that matter, how this group of users might be attracted to services. Reporting on the findings of a community survey of cocaine users, the majority of whom reported an opiate-using history, the authors recommend a service response combining the medical treatments offered by community drug teams with an accessible drop-in service and an outreach initiative of peer education, as an appropriate intervention for crack cocaine users.

Drugs workers and service providers in the current study expressed concern about increased availability and use of cocaine among their client groups. However, it also seems clear that some services are currently more likely than others to be treating clients who report the use of cocaine. Consequently, the lack of consensus on appropriate treatment and intervention responses to cocaine use is not altogether surprising. More critical perhaps, is the fact that drug workers felt that they lacked adequate knowledge and understanding of cocaine use among their client groups, including information on dominant user practices and the effects, risks and health consequences associated with the co-abuse of heroin and cocaine.

3.6 Exploratory Study of Social/Recreational Cocaine Use

Population surveys in Ireland identify few cocaine users. However, anecdotal evidence suggests that cocaine is easily available and its use more widespread than previously was the case. In this exploratory study of social/recreational cocaine use, the research challenge was to locate and gain the co-operation of a small number of adult cocaine users in the community, who are not currently attending, and who have at no stage contacted, a drug treatment centre. In other words, the emphasis was on accessing individuals who do not identify themselves as having a drug problem. The principal aim was to 'capture' users not normally accessible through treatment or other institutional settings and to examine patterns of use and attitudes to cocaine.

3.6.1 Study Parameters, Research Instruments and the Recruitment Process

The study's selection criteria, in terms of past and current cocaine use, was deliberately broad. No strict or binding guidelines pertaining to precise levels of drug intake were applied at the outset of the selection procedure, owing to the absence of prior empirical research on cocaine use in an Irish context. However, to qualify for participation in the study, respondents had to have used cocaine at least five times during their lifetime, preferably at least once during the past year. Other criteria for entry to the study, in addition to some experience with cocaine, were that participants must be 21 years of age or older and must have been employed for at least six of the twelve months prior to interview.

The purpose of the research was not to ascertain how many people use cocaine, but rather to gain some insight into reported patterns of cocaine use among a small group of social users. Hence, the central concern was not one of generalisability but one of access. In this context, the guiding principle was 'less is more' (McCracken, 1988:17). McCracken (1988), who describes the key characteristics of the long interview, recommends working longer and with greater care with a small number of people, and suggests that eight respondents are sufficient for many research projects.

The research aimed to generate knowledge and insight into cocaine use by adults not associated in problematic drug consumption, a phenomenon not previously researched in an Irish context. Ten adult cocaine users were interviewed in-depth during May/June 2000. The questions addressed in the context of individual interviews included how users first came into contact with cocaine, how their use progressed from the time of initial use, past and current cocaine use, how they regulated their intake of the drug, typical cocaine-using contexts, availability, cost and quality of cocaine, the benefits of cocaine, perceptions of risks associated with use, and the appeal of cocaine. Importantly, the research examined respondents' use of a range of mood-altering substances, so that cocaine was not examined in isolation from other drug use.

Study respondents were accessed initially via the researcher's personal contacts with potential participants. This gradually facilitated access to other individuals through 'snowballing', whereby, additional respondents were recruited through the recommendations of individuals previously interviewed. This technique is well-known in the drugs research field and is particularly suited to investigations of illicit and hidden activities (Biernacki & Waldorf, 1981; Power, 1989).

In an effort to access a range of cocaine-related experiences, attempts were made to contact a variety of user networks. The recruitment task proved more difficult than originally anticipated, particularly during the early stages of establishing contact with cocaine users. Prospective participants were sceptical about the intentions of the research and understandably reluctant to divulge details about their drug use. They invariably asked questions about the purpose of the study and about the publication of study findings. The challenges to recruitment were overcome by gradually extending access routes and by providing assurances of anonymity and confidentiality. The recommendations of key informants (individuals who had contact with cocaine users) greatly facilitated this process. The time invested in the selection of participants resulted in six user networks across the sample. All interviews were tape-recorded. Choice as to the time and place of the interview rested with the participant. Interviews took place in a variety of settings including the researcher's office (n=1) or home (n=1), a public venue (n=3) or at the home of the respondent (n=5).

Biographical details and drug history were recorded for each respondent using a pre-coded, structured questionnaire. This included details of each respondent's age, gender, education, employment, household situation and current income. Lifetime, past month and past week drug use, as well as future drug intentions, were recorded for each individual participant. All respondents resided in Dublin city. The study does not claim to be representative of social/recreational cocaine users generally. Rather, it is illustrative of a 'mode' of cocaine involvement among adults who do not consider their drug use to be problematic.

The protection of informants' identities was a priority throughout the research. No names, addresses or contact numbers were recorded on the pre-coded questionnaires. In addition, all identifiers (place names, birth place, current area of residence and so on) were removed from transcript material and fictitious names substituted in all cases for the purpose of reporting the study findings.

3.6.2 Data Analysis

Full transcripts of nine of the ten individual in-depth interviews were prepared. A partial transcript was prepared for one interview owing to poor conditions at the interview site, resulting in a high level of background noise. This partial transcript was reinforced by note-taking both during and after the interview. The findings presented here are based on a thematic analysis of all transcript material. Boyatzis (1998) describes thematic analysis as a 'process for encoding qualitative information' (Boyatzis, 1998: 4) and clarifies the meaning and use of themes for analytic purposes.

A theme is a pattern found in the information that at a minimum describes and organises the possible observations and at a maximum interprets aspects of the phenomenon.

(Boyatzis, 1998: 4)

In other words, a theme is not merely a 'fact' or set of facts extracted from the data but a pattern that presents itself throughout a data set. Themes provide a useful interpretative structure for understanding the phenomenon of interest. The data were coded manually in accordance with the research aims, and ancillary codes were added as the fieldwork process advanced. In this way, the analysis incorporated both predefined categories and those that emerged directly from respondents' accounts of their cocaine use.

Interpretation of the results has to be qualified by a number of study limitations. First, the research is based solely on self-reports of frequency and quantity of drug consumption of a small number of informants, all of whom were resident in Dublin city at the time of interview. Second, the sample was opportunistic or one of convenience. Accordingly, it would be inappropriate to generalise the findings to cocaine-using adults generally.

A number of techniques were employed throughout the data collection and analysis phases of the research to ensure valid and reliable findings. The safeguards concerning confidentiality and anonymity help to validate the responses. Moreover, the questioning and data collection techniques employed meant that the consistency of cocaine and other drug use reported by respondents could be checked. All respondents were asked about their drug use (lifetime, past month and past week use) on two separate occasions during the interview. This data were also recorded on a questionnaire. One hundred per cent consistency was found in respondents' reports in nearly all cases.

The presentation of research findings focuses, first, on the socio-demographic characteristics of study respondents. Baseline data on cocaine and other drug use are then presented. The analysis moves then to present a more detailed description of respondents' use of cocaine, including the circumstances surrounding use, the appeal of cocaine, the negative effects and perceived benefits of cocaine use and risk perceptions. The issues of availability, price and purity are also examined.

3.6.3 Socio-Demographic Characteristics

Eight males and two females were interviewed individually. The average age of the research respondents was 27.3 years (range 25-29 years). Nine of the ten interviewees were born in Ireland. One was born in the United Kingdom but had been residing in Ireland for several years.

The educational attainment for the sample was high. All had completed their Leaving Certificate or equivalent and all attended a third-level educational institution. Eight of the ten respondents graduated with a third-level degree or diploma. At the time of the interview, eight were employed full-time and two part-time. All had experienced periods of unemployment ranging from two months to six years. It is significant, however, that in most cases, stated periods of unemployment coincided with time spent travelling abroad and extended for between one and two years. Two respondents declined to state their current gross annual income. Of the eight who did, annual incomes ranged from £10,000 to £30,000. Seven of the ten respondents were earning in excess of £20,000 per annum and five had a gross annual income of between £25,000 and £30,000.

Finally, all respondents resided in Dublin city. All were single and over half (n=6) lived with a partner. Three respondents lived with friends and one with her child. All respondents resided in a rented private-sector house or apartment.

3.6.4 Patterns of Cocaine Use and Routes of Administration

This section provides baseline data on the respondents' reported cocaine use. The average age of initiation into cocaine use was 21.2 years and half (n=5) reported first use between the ages of 20 and 23 years. On average, respondents had a cocaine 'career' of 6.5 years since initiation. Eight of the ten respondents had used cocaine at least once during the month preceding the interview. The most popular mode of cocaine ingestion was 'snorting', or intranasal use of the drug. Two respondents reported having ingested the drug orally on a number of occasions and a third stated that he had smoked cocaine in a 'joint'. This was the only reported method of smoking cocaine. In fact, the majority were not familiar with the practice of 'freebasing' and did not regard this mode of administration as a future drug option.

Cocaine typologies have been devised by several researchers, based on participants' reported frequency and intensity of use (Hammersley & Ditton, 1994; Waldorf et al., 1991; Ditton, Hammersley, Philips, Forsyth & Khan, 1996).

This technique was not utilised in the current study owing to the small sample size. However, it is helpful to summarise general patterns of cocaine use for the sample. Following initiation, the majority did engage in subsequent use for some time (in some cases, for two to three years). Overall patterns of cocaine use varied considerably across the sample. Although a number (n=4) reported bingeing on cocaine, the duration of such 'bouts' of use were short, and most (n=6) had not used cocaine for more than two consecutive days. Monthly use emerged as the most frequently-reported current pattern of use; daily cocaine use was not the norm for this group of users. Nine of the ten respondents intended to use cocaine in the future. The remaining participant stated that she may well use cocaine at some time but had no definite plans to do so in the immediate future.

3.6.5 Other Drug Use

Practically all respondents were experienced users of a range of illegal drugs. Table 3.11 presents the figures for lifetime, past month and past week use of cocaine and other drugs. Drug intentions are also included on this table. Alcohol and tobacco, being licit drugs, are referred to independently. Six of the ten respondents were current smokers and all consumed alcohol on a regular (two to three times weekly) basis.

TABLE 3.11.
Lifetime, Recent and Future Use of Cocaine and Other Drugs (n=10).

Drug	Lifetime Use	Past Month Use	Past Week Use	Future Drug Use*
Cannabis	10	10	8	10
Ecstasy	10	7	4	7
LSD	10	1	1	2
Amphetamine	10	0	0	1
Cocaine	10	8	4	9
Heroin	3	0	0	0
Methadone	2	0	0	0
Magic Mushrooms/ Psilocybin	9	0	0	3
Glue/Solvents	2	0	0	0
Tranquillisers	3	0	0	0
Other	6	0	0	0

Respondents were asked to state which drugs they intended to use in the future.

The average age of drug initiation for the sample was 15.8 years (range 13 to 19 years). Five respondents were 17 years or over at the time of first drug use. Table 3.11 indicates that respondents had tried or used a range of substances. All reported lifetime use of cannabis, ecstasy, LSD and amphetamine. Nine had used magic mushrooms (psilocybin). Three respondents reported lifetime use of heroin; two had used methadone; two tranquillisers; and two solvents or inhalants at some stage. Lifetime use of other substances not listed included opium (n=2), mescaline (n=2) and 'crystal meths' (methamphetamine) (n=2).

Cannabis was by far the most commonly-stated drug of initiation, and LSD and psilocybin (magic mushrooms) were frequently-stated second drugs used (n=7). Seven of the ten respondents were regular cannabis users (weekly or fortnightly users) and a significant number (n=6) reported past month use of ecstasy. A large number reported concurrent drug use, that is, the use of two or more substances in close succession for the attainment of specific or heightened drug experiences. The most popular drug cocktails were alcohol and cocaine; alcohol and cannabis; ecstasy and cannabis; cocaine, ecstasy and cannabis; and ecstasy and cocaine. Cannabis was considered to be compatible with most drugs and was frequently smoked subsequent to the ingestion of another substance. Nearly half the respondents (n=4) reported daily or near-daily use of cannabis.

Nine respondents intended to use cannabis and cocaine at some stage in the future and a large number expected to use ecstasy (n=7). Considerably fewer intended to use LSD (n=2), psilocybin (n=2) or amphetamine (n=1).

3.6.6 First Use of Cocaine

Respondents were asked to describe the circumstances surrounding their initial use of cocaine. In practically all cases, use was initiated in the company of friends in a social setting where alcohol and/or other drugs were being consumed. The majority stated that they had contemplated cocaine use in advance of first experimentation. However, while most stated that they intended to try cocaine at some stage, first use usually occurred incidentally. For this reason, first cocaine experiences were often free.

> *With friends at a party under the influence of another drug which was Ecstasy. I hadn't planned it as such but I had expressed an interest in taking it before that night anyway. I was up and ready for it but I hadn't planned it.*

I was with some other musicians and they had it. It's a social drug and they were sharing it. At that time I was only starting to dabble with that kind of stuff. Someone asked me did I want some so I tried it.

For a smaller number of respondents (n=3), first cocaine use involved some advance planning.

I got it through friends. I asked to get it. I got it for a party. And I was in my early 20s at the time, about twenty-two.

At the time of initiation, most shared approximately one gram of cocaine with two or three friends, the typical intake being 'two or three lines' or 'a few lines'. Informants frequently reported drinking alcohol and/or using one other drug (either cannabis or ecstasy) at the time of initial cocaine use. The majority reported first cocaine experiences in positive terms.

It was amazing. Down there (abroad) anytime I got it, it was absolutely amazing. I could really see the attraction in it ... it was weird being so high but so clear. I suppose it was a very confident buzz I got out of it.

I thoroughly enjoyed it, yes it was good. It has similarities to other stimulants as such but I would certainly differentiate between that and ecstasy or speed.

Only one respondent stated that he was not impressed with the drug at the time of first use and asserted that he 'didn't really see what the attraction was'. Most agreed that subsequent cocaine experiences were superior to first or early use episodes. A process of learning to recognise and appreciate cocaine effects clearly accompanied the initial stages of use.

I remember being able to deal with it and just kind of recognise the buzz and again it was probably just a learning thing going on.

There is not a huge kick off it [cocaine] which is why I think you don't know what to expect at first and maybe after the second time you probably ... you can tell people 'that was crap' and they say 'well, did you not feel this' ... and then you say, 'well maybe I did'. And then the next time you have probably talked yourself into the buzz, what you are supposed to feel.

At the time of first use, practically all respondents had previously experimented with and used a range of stimulant and hallucinogenic drugs. In fact, cocaine was commonly listed as fifth or sixth drug ever used. On average, there was a five-and-a-half-year time lapse between first drug use and first cocaine use. Hence, the majority were 'experienced' drug-takers at the time they first tried cocaine. None expressed any doubt, scepticism or anxiety about the prospect of using cocaine when describing the circumstances surrounding first use of the drug. Hence, although cocaine initiation occurred later in respondents' drug 'careers', it was not an unexpected or unanticipated event.

3.6.7 Frequency and Contexts of Cocaine Use

All respondents were asked explicit questions about the frequency and quantity of their cocaine use generally. However, during questioning, there was a particular focus on two specific periods - use during the two-to-three-year period subsequent to initiation, and cocaine consumption during the two years preceding the interview. Hence, early and current use of the drug were examined in detail, in order to construct typical patterns of cocaine use across time. Given the substantial drug history of respondents prior to first cocaine use, coupled with frequent reports of using cocaine in association with alcohol and other substances, cocaine use is examined here with reference to respondents' use of a range of substances. This section will describe respondents' cocaine use, in terms of the frequency, intensity, intake and duration of use. The circumstances and locations associated with use are important components of this analysis.

As stated earlier, there was a considerable time-lapse between first and more regular use of cocaine. Hence, while cocaine initiation took place, on average, at the age of 21, more consistent use of the drug did not emerge for quite some time. Use of the drug was sporadic initially, and appeared to be dictated largely by economic factors: cocaine was expensive and most respondents had not yet secured their first job. Availability was an additional factor that appeared to deter regular use at this stage.

> In those days I was a student and I had fuck all money anyway, you know. And a lot of the time when you're in that scenario, you probably get in with somebody and get to know somebody who has a contact somewhere else. Or, they might be dealing themselves or be able to get it irregularly or cheaply. And coke wasn't one of those kinds of drugs that you could get easily. And when you got it, it was never cheap.

When I was 21, £80 or £70 for a wrap of coke plus your drinking, plus getting into a club ... I just couldn't do it. £150 out of your pocket for a night, I just couldn't do it ... and I wouldn't have had it myself because I wouldn't really have known the people that you would get it from, so it would have been a real hit and miss thing which will change as you go along because you will find people who sell it.

Consequently, early use of cocaine was intermittent and viewed largely as a 'treat', or an extravagant drug for special occasions. At this stage, other drugs were more likely than cocaine to be in use, largely because they were more economical and easier to procure.

I'd say it was more sporadic [for several years after first use], you know. If it was available and if I had the money in my pocket I'd get it. But if there was other stuff available I wouldn't bother. I'd go the cheap route because number one it's [other drugs] cheaper and number two, it'll go further.

There were huge gaps between when I would take it, so it would be months between taking it. It could be two or three months before a similar party or circumstance would come up. But it was always party generated, you know, because of the nature of it.

It is significant that among this group of informants, in their mid- to late-twenties, most had only started to use cocaine more regularly during the past three years or less. Current frequency of use varied across the group. The largest number (n=7) reported monthly use of cocaine. One stated that he had used cocaine approximately eight times during the past year. For two others, use was less regular and less deliberate: some respondents did not secure a regular personal supply of the drug and described their current use as occasional.

It is very rarely an arranged thing. It would be a case of somebody saying 'I have two grams of coke, does anyone want to go in on it?' That is probably the extent of my cocaine use at the moment. I wouldn't be a huge fan, I don't really see the value in it, shall we say.

One respondent reported having reduced her cocaine intake from former, more regular and intense consumption levels, including two 'bouts' of use when she used cocaine several times weekly.

Given that regular cocaine use was quite a recent development for the majority of respondents, it is important to examine how they described this drug transition. As stated previously, all respondents reported a sizeable repertoire of drugs prior to cocaine initiation. A large number were current, regular cannabis users. In addition, practically all had gone through a short phase of LSD use and a sustained phase of ecstasy use, ranging from several months to two years. While ecstasy was described in positive terms, the majority drew attention to the negative effects of regular, heavy use and indicated a definite shift from this particular 'style' of ecstasy use. Most stated that while they currently used ecstasy on occasions, they had quit regular weekend use of the drug.

> I don't do E that often any more. I used to alright but, ah, just too much hassle now with the come down an' all. But yeah, I used to love it and would still do it but not in the way I used to. Takes too long to recover.

> I haven't done any [E] for a long time. It is so physically draining for me to take, you know, you take an E and for a couple of days you are just not really as sharp as you normally should be. You are not really on the ball. It takes an awful lot out of you. I haven't taken acid in a couple of years either and that's the same, it knocks you for six.

Many perceived cocaine to be a lighter, more manageable drug. First, cocaine did not induce powerful physical effects during use, certainly compared to ecstasy. Second, it did not produce profound negative side-effects during the days following use. Both factors emerged as primary motives for a reduction of ecstasy (and LSD) intake on the one hand, and increased cocaine use on the other.

> I know if it is a line or two of coke I still find I can go about my daily routine. If I take ecstasy I know I won't feel the best the next day but Es are a funny thing. Sometimes you take one and you find that you can be in a pub atmosphere, enjoy a pint or two and its not too heavy. And then sometimes you take another and whatever is in it, you're just gone.

> In comparison to ecstasy, physically with ecstasy it is hard to get up the next day and get through it, you know, you have black rings under your eyes. Usually on ecstasy you're higher than you are on cocaine, even if it is really good cocaine. And then mentally with ecstasy, you know sometimes you have to have a couple of days to recover from the night out as such. Coke does not have that effect, not on me anyway. It is far easier to just go out and have a good time with some coke and get up the next day and either go to work or just get through the day and not be in a hassle.

Respondents' preferred circumstances of cocaine use varied but most favoured a relaxed setting in the company of friends. Respondents regularly drew attention to the circumstances of use and considered the setting to be a strong determinant of positive drug experiences.

> *Sometimes the buzz with coke is a bit better than others because of purity I suppose. But it is 90 per cent circumstances. I am not saying that circumstances completely override the quality of coke at the end of the day, you know, if you are a relatively seasoned user. But at the end of the day when I look back at nights when I have taken coke or taken some other drug it is usually the circumstances and the company that I keep and whether I am enjoying myself, and my current state of mind. They are usually the predominant factors in how good the night was, you know.*

A majority preferred to use cocaine in private, rather than public, social settings. Situations in which people wished to communicate and enjoy the company of friends were most frequently mentioned as those where cocaine use occurred. Less frequent, but visible also, were situations in which people wanted to dance.

> *I prefer to use coke in a house. Yes, with a few friends in the house. I have used it in clubs before but you wouldn't be using there often because you can't use it openly, you know.*

> *It would be mostly at home or in the pub you might slip into the jacks and have a quickie in the coke sense. But generally it would be in a house situation. It is not really conducive to doing in a public place in that there is a little bit of preparation and that involved. You have to get it out into a line and it is not the ready-made package that our friend ecstasy is.*

> *I'd be inclined to use cocaine in quieter more laid back circumstances ... say there was a weekend of music somewhere, a festival or something like that. I'd make up my mind, like I'd go for coke or for a few tablets as well, you know.*

> *Taken on its own [cocaine] you are elated and you are aware of yourself but you are aware of yourself as being full of confidence and you feel really sexy and especially say, if you are dancing or you are in a club.*

Most respondents reported using cocaine in a social setting at night-time (either at home or out). However, a small number had also used cocaine during the day on occasions, although this was by no means a preferred or usual practice.

The last time I took coke was two weeks ago. It was in the middle of the day and I was sitting in. I was away for a week and I was sitting in the house drinking cups of coffee and smoking joints. And we decided it was time to hit the town so it was about mid-afternoon, something like that. And I had a line, went out, spent the whole day buzzing around and would have had maybe two or three more lines that night.

From the reports of respondents it could be inferred that cocaine use is strongly related to lifestyles where going out, social gatherings and socialising are dominant. For the most part, cocaine use was confined to weekends and holiday times, when there was sufficient time to 'recover' and fewer potential negative repercussions from use or over-indulgence. In addition, cocaine use was strongly linked with alcohol consumption. A number of respondents commented on the compatibility of alcohol and cocaine. In fact, cocaine was rarely, if ever, consumed alone. Although descriptions of use varied, cocaine-using scenarios invariably incorporated the use of other mood-altering substances, including cannabis, alcohol and, less frequently, ecstasy.

It is a drug you tend to mix as well, primarily with alcohol now, the two, for whatever reason seem to combine. Now medically they could be the worst thing for you, I don't know, but from a results or effects point of view they mix well and you tend to drink more and you tend to sit around and you would be in considerably better form, not really sure why, considerably better form.

Coke and alcohol are a very crucial mix for a night. If you are doing coke you have to have some booze so I would say that that goes hand in hand with the amount of booze you are going to go through.

Hash may or may not come into it as well. If we're out drinking and are back in someone's house we might have a smoke or not. I actually like mixing ecstasy with a bit of coke too, you know it's good fun. You get a good energy and physical [pause], an energetic rush from the ecstasy both mentally and physically and taking it with a bit of coke also maintains the same kind of rush that you would have got from ecstasy. So it is almost prolonging the effect that you get from ecstasy. They are both stimulants so they are both doing the same kind of thing but ecstasy makes you more amorous and friendly to others and you would be less likely to talk about yourself.

Current frequency of use was strongly linked with economic factors. Individuals with more disposable income were far more likely to use monthly or weekly. One respondent stated that cocaine was simply not economical and that he could not afford to buy the drug regularly. Compared to other drugs, cocaine's short-lived effects relative to its high cost rendered other drug choices more cost-effective.

> For the same money, if you want to compare them as regards what the user gets out of it, you get a much better night or a much better hit of six Es which is the equivalent [cost wise] as a gram of coke. It think it [cocaine] is very expensive and prohibitively expensive which is probably a good thing because if it got any cheaper, it would become a lot more popular very quickly because I have noticed an increase in its popularity in the last year, year and a half.

> On a scale of drugs that I'd take, it would probably be the least common drug that I'd use. Um, because for value for money, it's the worst. Because you could actually buy a gram and consume the whole gram in one night. So that's eighty quid, gone, whack. Whereas you could get a good quality ecstasy tablet for a tenner that would last you the whole night. So, it's down the list for me anyway.

Other respondents, by contrast, stated that their current income permitted more regular use of cocaine than in the past.

> Well, at first it was never really something that I went out of my way to go off and take and then when I had a bit more disposable income and I was growing tired of other drugs that I had taken, ecstasy really, then I started doing it a bit more.

> As a young adult I couldn't really afford it whereas now I can afford it so there is that sort of thing.

One respondent attributed his increased cocaine consumption during the past year to a heavy workload, resulting in more stress and fatigue.

> It [cocaine intake] has probably increased a little this year. I don't know why really? Probably work because I am working a hell of a lot more and so, I would have two nights off. And I kind of go for it big, kind of a more intense night out. And that is probably one of the reasons for it. Plus, in the last few months ... it gives you that sort of a pick up. Because at the moment I have changed job so I am working more hours and am more tired.

The study's regular users of cocaine generally restricted use to weekends, when their intake of the drug ranged between one and two grams per session. Most reported periods of abstinence ranging from one to several months. While a number of informants stated that there were times when they had exceeded their usual intake, bingeing on cocaine was not a common practice. Cocaine was rarely used on more than two consecutive days.

> *I suppose in the past I may have taken a load of coke and not slept, had a meal or something like that and then started a session again if there was a particular reason to be on a party buzz. And then I may have done it two nights in a row, sometimes I suppose three but I have never gone on a complete weekender without any sleep.*

> *I've never actually taken coke for more than like two days or something like that. I've never gone on a binge of coke.*

One respondent did report two separate phases of intense and regular cocaine use. On both occasions, the individual had easy access to the drug and did not have to pay a high price for a 'good' supply.

> *I have gone on coke sprees. I remember one in particular and it was really, really good. About three years ago it was with my boyfriend's friend. He had loads of it and it was pure and when I think about that, it is interesting because now that I remember it, it was great because there wasn't any comedown. I think I have particularly bad comedowns because of what it is mixed with. But he was giving us the good stuff.*

To summarise, while frequency of cocaine use varied across the ten respondents, it was possible to identify a number of distinct patterns of use. The largest group of cocaine users (n=5) had previously used a range of other stimulants (ecstasy and amphetamine) and hallucinogenic drugs (LSD and magic mushrooms) and had significantly curbed their intake of these substances. Respondents regularly drew attention to the cumulative negative effects of sustained ecstasy use and to the lengthy recovery period following use. In this context, cocaine had increasingly emerged as a drug of choice. This shift also appeared to coincide with significant lifestyle changes. In particular, respondents reported increased career commitments. Importantly, this group of mid- to relatively high-earners had more disposable income than previously. Cocaine was considered to be a 'cleaner' drug, and use did not impinge on routine responsibilities, which centred largely on professional and career considerations. This sub-group engaged predominantly in weekend cocaine use, with frequency of use varying between one and four times monthly.

Four additional respondents described a pattern of less regular cocaine use. This group's drug preferences did not focus as strongly on cocaine and they reported more regular use of other drugs. While cocaine-using occasions were sometimes planned, most occurred by chance. For this group, cocaine was not a primary drug of use and was more likely to be used intermittently and incorporated into a wider poly-drug repertoire. Finally, one participant, a former regular cocaine user, had not used cocaine for several months.

In general terms, the broad picture emerging of the study respondents is one of eclectic poly-drug use. It appears that cocaine has become a more regular and valued feature of this group's poly-drug 'careers'. Regularity of cocaine use varied across the sample and use frequency appeared to be determined by a number of interacting factors including past drug experiences, current income and user's drug preferences.

3.6.8 Availability, Purity and Price of Cocaine

Respondents were asked to comment on current availability and ease of cocaine accessibility. Across the sample, there was general consensus that cocaine was more easily available and more commonly used than previously.

It is far more freely available now, you would see more and more types of people doing it and there are bars and clubs in town where a lot of people would use it ... it would have had that tag of being a more exclusive drug years ago because it wasn't freely available and used more for an occasion. But now a lot more people I know do it every weekend.

It's a lot easier to get it now really, but that's probably down to my own circle of acquaintances as well. Yeah, if I want it I can get it.

Coupled with increased availability, there was a strong belief in cocaine's acceptance as a drug of choice.

There is a large acceptance, people that I know and people's parents do it the odd time, do a line, and it is fine by them.

There is a big difference now, sure even if you look at toilets in a club, it is nothing to see two males go in and out of a cubicle together and the likelihood is that they are both going in to do a line but nobody bats an eyelid. I think years ago whereby we were told how bad drugs were, people would readily stand up and go 'listen'. That is not on nowadays. There just doesn't seem to be that anymore. Nobody is going to turn around and be disgusted that you are doing something like that.

Strong differences emerged, however, in the perceived reliability of personal access routes to cocaine. Expectations regarding the quality and purity of available supplies also varied. Regular cocaine users had sought out and located one or more reliable supplier of the drug and felt assured about the quality of cocaine they purchased.

I find availability okay. I wouldn't buy it off somebody I didn't know, and you are still taking a bit of a gamble with somebody you know with what you are getting, you are still not getting extremely good quality but I would have no problems, if I got muck in cocaine, giving it back to the person [supplier] as well. I wouldn't pay that amount for something that's not acceptable at all.

Others, who did not have a regular dealer, relied on friends to secure a supply of cocaine. It appeared that those who socialised in user circuits were able to access cocaine easily.

If I wanted it [cocaine] I would have to talk to a particular friend ... and he would talk to the guy who deals it for him. I don't have a dealer so if I heard there was something going on at the weekend and people getting stuff I could ring up and just say put me down for a wrap [a single quantity, usually 1 gram] or whatever.

Less committed and regular users of the drug, on the other hand, had to go to greater lengths to procure 'good' cocaine and a number did not have a reliable dealer.

I have a regular supplier for years and I wouldn't be a heavy coke user. So anytime I go to get coke, it's more of a hassle for me to go and get it because I have to go out of my way to get it because he doesn't supply it.

The quality varies from very poor to very good. Again, there is no trend to that either, it's totally pot luck. I am sure there are people, and again this is my experience because I don't know many people or one person, to be honest, who sells the stuff. If you knew more people that sold it, the chances are you would probably be able to get it more regularly and get good stuff.

Respondents' reports indicate that the current street price of cocaine varies between £50 and £80 per gram. The majority stated that the quality and purity of supplies vary enormously depending on the source and availability of the drug. Most respondents had used cocaine while in countries other than Ireland at some stage and frequently mentioned the inferior quality of cocaine here, certainly compared to that which they had sampled abroad.

> *The way you kind of socially create sources for obtaining coke, well after a while you do notice that one person gives you coke and it may not be as good as the next person. And sometimes after a few years or after a while of taking it you can actually take some lines of coke and you can actually see what it is cut with, you can taste it or you can see it. It is just something that you develop over the course of time and the purity in Dublin anyway is not always the best.*

> *It is pricey, but as well as that you see it is hard to tell because in Ireland it is hard to get good cocaine. You can get it but it is few and far between, it is a bit of a gamble when you go to buy because you don't know if it's going to be good. But if you have a regular source and you know what is good then you are fine. And you will find that there are times when you will get really good stuff all the time and then other times you are getting crap, you know.*

In general, the evidence suggests that cocaine is readily accessible to individuals who are motivated to use the drug and have established contact with a reliable supplier. Less frequent users, while having easy access to cannabis and ecstasy via their regular dealers, had less well established access routes to illicit cocaine supply systems. They were not motivated to seek out a more reliable cocaine supply route and allowed situational factors to determine the quality of the cocaine they consumed. At the buyer level then, it would appear that cocaine, albeit of variable quality, is relatively easily available to individuals who opt to use the drug.

3.6.9 Perceived Attractive and Unattractive Aspects of Cocaine

All psychoactive substances have appealing and unattractive attributes and cocaine is no exception in this regard. All of the respondents were well versed on the drug-induced outcomes of a variety of substances; they distinguished clearly between the effects of individual drugs and had preferences for specific drugs or drug combinations, depending on the circumstances or settings of use. In this section, the perceived appealing and negative aspects of cocaine are examined. Reference is made to the perceived advantages of other drugs in instances where this has a bearing on respondents' attitude to cocaine.

The data revealed three dominant cocaine attractions. They are not discussed here in hierarchical order, as it was difficult to determine individual advantages which prevailed over others in terms of their importance for individual users. Rather, all three merged as components of a psychoactive 'hit' which was perceived to be gratifying, beneficial and enjoyable. Cocaine's appeal focused on three major themes - pleasure, control and lifestyle.

Cocaine simply made partying better, according to the majority of respondents. The psychoactive 'hit' produced feelings of exhilaration, confidence and psychological pleasure, thus enhancing social occasions in which the drug was in use.

> *Taken on its own you are elated and you are really aware of everything and you are aware of yourself but you are aware of yourself as being full of confidence.*

> *It boosts the night by about five-fold. If you are out and you are having a great laugh it seems to add that little bit extra to the night. The banter is a bit quicker as it goes on ... It is just like a mood enhancer.*

> *With coke you can have a little stash of it and you can stay up all night. It is just that it breaks down all those barriers and you are just babbling away having a good time, socialising with people.*

Closely linked to the social and psychological pleasures described by respondents was that cocaine provided an immediate injection of energy and enthusiasm and made the night last longer.

> *If I was taking uppers - speed, cocaine, something like that - it would be to promote my energy levels for the evening or elongate it so you can go with the craic for longer.*

Two respondents drew attention to the enhancement of sexual experiences following cocaine use.

> *Coke is more of an indoor drug and if you are with someone that you are quite into a relationship with it is good as well. You can lock yourself in and have a gram of coke and have a really good night sexually as well as mentally.*

As with other drugs, the pleasure factor was high on respondents' list of priorities when rating cocaine as a drug experience. The physical and psychological pleasures cited by respondents in the current study are very similar to those documented by Ditton et al. (1996) in their sample of cocaine users in Scotland.

A second key advantage of cocaine over other drugs, according to many informants, was that unlike other drugs, cocaine permitted the user to retain a high level of 'control' during times of use. Discretion was closely associated with control: cocaine did not demand much preparation and users felt able to conceal the fact that they had taken the drug. In addition, cocaine consumption facilitated and enhanced communication with others, rather than hampering it. At the same time, the rapid onset of cocaine-induced effects following consumption, coupled with the short duration of these effects, allowed the user to maintain charge over his/her disposition and behaviour.

> It's immediately effective and it's convenient to carry around and it's convenient to take, relatively. Like, there's no work, you don't have to prepare anything, you know. And you get an immediate kick out of it.

> You can control it insofar as it only lasts ten minutes and then you can take some more of it if you want it. Whereas ecstasy, you take it and you are out of it for at least two hours.

> It is the most social because you can sit there and you can converse with everyone and you don't look like you are out of it. It's a good drug like that.

> It doesn't stop me thinking and I don't do anything stupid, you know what I mean. You can get into a taxi and talk to the taxi man and you know what you're doing.

Critically, cocaine use, according to several respondents, did not result in the negative after-effects associated with ecstasy and other drugs. These included physical and/or psychological exhaustion and feelings of being 'wrecked' during the days following use. Half the respondents (n=5) reported several undesirable side-effects following a sustained period of regular ecstasy use. Cocaine, on the other hand, did not give rise to feelings of physical or psychological exhaustion, or feelings of being 'wrecked', during the days following use. It appears that, compared to other drugs, several respondents felt more 'control' over their physical and psychological condition following cocaine use.

> *If you do acid or ecstasy the next day you are feeling a bit rough physically, a couple of days later you may be feeling a bit depressed or even the day after doing it you are lacking in energy and lacking in lustre in general. The advantages of cocaine for the user would be that in comparison to other drugs, the next day you are grand. Well, you might have a bit of a head on you but nothing that a shower and a fry wouldn't pretty much cure.*

> *I have really gone off ecstasy just with mood swings during the week from it. And there was a time, I think, when I probably would have preferred ecstasy but at the moment if I was to go out I would probably say no to ecstasy and see coke as a lot lighter. I don't feel as bad the next day so I would probably do a bit of coke. Maybe I'm getting old! I'm not really able for it anymore and the high just isn't worth it, the low now outweighs the high.*

Respondents' need to function clearly, in the context of maintaining a valued career, was closely linked with cocaine's appeal and the perceived absence of serious and costly after-effects. Cocaine use did not encroach on the user's ability to carry out work-related responsibilities efficiently. Hence, it allowed the user to maintain a lifestyle where work played a central role.

> *I like the fact that you can go out and have a really good night, have a blast and then the next day you can carry on and you can function properly and go to work and do your job. You don't want to just go in and be useless for the day because one day lost is bad really.*

Despite cocaine's notoriety as the 'champagne of drugs', few respondents overtly referred to cocaine's traditional association with the rich and famous. However, subtle references were made to cocaine's glamorous image and its acceptability within particular social circles.

> *I think in terms of image it is definitely viewed as, it is almost always viewed as glamorous. Of all of them [other drugs] it is probably associated with rock and film stars. So, I think it has a very glamorous image.*

> *Initially, especially, it was that kind of feeling, maybe a little bit of superiority in a sense because you had it [cocaine] and it can become part of your evening. And yet other*

people aren't doing it and it kind of sets you on a different level to some people and that is some of the attraction of it.

Respondents drew attention to relatively few negative aspects of cocaine use, certainly, compared to the range of perceived positive attributes. Cost emerged as the dominant disadvantage of cocaine use and, for a considerable number, this was a key factor deterring regular use. In addition to cost, cocaine's unpredictability, in terms of the quality and purity of supplies, meant there was a significant risk of getting a 'bad deal'. Other drugs were more reliable and considered to be better value in terms of the nature and duration of the resulting psychoactive 'hit'.

My experience of cocaine is that it's very much potluck and that could mean £60 or £70 down the tubes ... it's too expensive, it really is like.

In terms of how cocaine rates here, I wouldn't rate it that highly at all because I'd have, I know I can get much better quality stuff that would give me a similar buzz, or better, for cheaper.

Four of the ten respondents described cocaine as a 'greedy drug'. When asked to elaborate on this statement, some drew attention to the user's desire to recreate the original 'high'. Others described scenarios where they had noticed people (friends and acquaintances) behaving in a self-indulgent way during sessions of use.

It is physical and it is mental. What happens when you are taking it is, with the first few lines that is when you feel you are most high. And then usually after that you are trying to recreate that high and what happens is that the process is [pause] ... anyway you want to recreate that buzz that you originally got and that may take a bit more than you originally took, if you follow me. And therein lies one aspect of the greed.

It is strange to see people with it [cocaine], it is a very greedy drug. I have never found it that way and maybe because I see everyone else being so greedy I tend not to be. And they slip off [for an extra line]. I hate to be like that. I suppose I have been disappointed in a few people, in their behaviour on it.

I have been at parties where, let's say, two or three or four people bought a gram of coke each. It is down on the mirror and it is there and you all set out having a nice line. And

*the next minute everyone is watching everyone else in case they nip in and get a line
ahead of them. So it can speed things up ... because you don't want to miss a line.*

When respondents were asked if they had experienced negative side-effects
following cocaine use, a number (n=3) stated that they had, at times, experienced
irritability and agitation.

*On one or two occasions there when I did too much of it I was lying there with my heart
pounding and then I must say it was a bit scary.*

*I think that the more you take of coke, the more irritable you become. In a physical sense,
like you'll actually get quite nervous as you go. So, there are some side-effects with the
use of the drug that would say, prey on your nervous system. I don't know? I've found
that, you know. If I took four lines in one night, I'd probably start feeling very kind of,
what's the word I'm looking for? Not nervous. Edgy, yeah. For me anyway, if I took
more than four lines of coke in a night I'd be feeling fairly edgy.*

One respondent stated that while on a positive note, cocaine induces strong
feelings of self-confidence, this can also prompt an undesirable overly-assertive
attitude on the part of the user.

*It gives you that kind of feeling that you have a stronger presence and you hold better
eye contact. You are very direct about what you are saying but at the same time that
can roll on to being quite aggressive. And I have had nights out where I have had
arguments about the most ridiculous things but I was right! And then you go home and
think, 'Jesus Christ, what was I talking about?'.*

In general, negative cocaine effects, including irritability, arrogance or
aggression, were attributed largely to having exceeded one's usual intake of the
drug. Since this was not a regular occurrence, it only qualified as a minor
irritation.

A small number of less regular users claimed that they had observed
unappealing behaviour in others who used the drug regularly and considered
cocaine to be an individualistic and egotistical drug. Their observations had led
them to conclude that, among some users, cocaine encouraged self-indulgent
and assuming behaviour. Others drew attention to mood swings and depression
among regular users.

I am talking about people I know and people who would use it as their drug of choice and not just on weekends, but on a regular basis. And it has changed them hugely. Like, you know, mood swings, vicious mood swings, and basically just depressed when they are not high on coke. And it makes for a sad life.

To summarise, cocaine was regarded as superior to other drugs for a variety of reasons. Users' subjective experiences suggest that cocaine was viewed positively by the majority of respondents. From the vantage point of the user, attractive features of cocaine included its energising effects, the ability to maintain control while intoxicated and the sociability of the drug. Cocaine was perceived to be a 'clean' drug, one that did not carry the negative image or undesirable after-effects of other stimulant drugs. Perhaps surprisingly, in view of cocaine's apparent allure, only two respondents described cocaine as their 'favourite' drug. Cannabis was by far the most popular drug across the sample (n=6). Two respondents stated that their preferred drug was ecstasy, in tablet or powder form.

3.6.10 Risk Perceptions and Self-Regulation of Cocaine Intake

Respondents were asked to express their views on the risks associated with cocaine and other drug use. In general, respondents had no reservations about using cocaine, provided they felt relatively self-assured about the source of the drug. Most stated that they would avoid buying cocaine from a stranger in social settings such as nightclubs. However, concerns about getting bad value for money tended to be higher on respondents' risk agenda, than anxieties about the presence of contaminants. Hence, one of the biggest 'risks' with cocaine was the unpredictability of available supplies and the gamble taken in this regard. Other drugs were considered to be far more reliable in this respect.

Cocaine isn't dodgy. You would probably be more likely to get a bad E that makes you ill for whatever reason. You will get bad coke but it is poor quality as opposed to anything else. When it's cut sometimes you can taste the glucose. E is probably more dangerous in that sense.

One respondent compared cocaine to legal substances when expressing his view on the risk of getting substandard cocaine.

I don't wonder what's in a cocktail at a bar because it's so readily available and acceptable. With cocaine it doesn't come into my head either, to be honest.

The overwhelming view was that cocaine was a 'safe' drug.

I think it's probably one of the safest drugs. You can't, of all the drugs that you can take, if you take acid there is a small chance that you will have a bad trip. But I think that cocaine is the safest drug. The effects are short-lived. There will only be ill-effects if you are doing it all the time but that won't happen easily because of the price of it.

When asked about the addictive potential of cocaine and other drugs, several respondents placed a great deal of emphasis on the individual's relationship with any given substance (including alcohol) as a major determinant of later difficulties. The general belief was that the pharmacological properties of the substance played a secondary role in the development of drug-related problems, certainly compared to other factors. This group of cocaine users did not consider that their own behaviour around drugs was comparable to the behaviour, personal or social conditions of individuals who experience drug problems.

I'd say it depends on your personality or your state of mind. But I could easily imagine if you're in a scenario whereby you have an altered state of being, by being on a drug, and your life is a piece of shit, well, you'll obviously going to get back to where you were last night as soon as possible. Now that depends on probably, your state of mind, your education, your ignorance of drugs. All of that, all those levels - your social circumstances, the amount of friends you have around you. If you feel lonely and you feel down, you know, you just more than likely want to get off your head. I could easily see somebody getting addicted to any drug. But specifically to cocaine? I don't know? I think if it was me I'd want to be seriously fucked in the head to get addicted to cocaine.

I can see why people can get addicted and having said that I could never see myself becoming an addict to coke. About a year and a half ago I kicked cigarettes and I think that is about as addictive as anything you can get.

Many pointed out that their use of cocaine and other drugs took place in social settings where friendships and other social relationships took precedence over the use, per se, of any drug. Respondents distinguished clearly between drug use and drug abuse, and did not equate their own cocaine use with dangerous or addictive patterns of drug consumption. Again, 'control' emerged as an organising construct in the discourse and respondents invariably pointed out that they, and not the drug, maintained 'charge' in the context of drug-taking scenarios.

I enjoy the fact that I have a fairly stable and happy atmosphere in my head and I am confident that I can do it [cocaine]. And if I ever felt that being threatened then there'd be no argument there. If it retarded my sense of drive or whatever, that'd be it.

I like to have control and I know how much I can handle. Yeah, I've overdone it at times but at the end of the day, drugs aren't important enough to me to let things get out of hand.

Several respondents recognised situations and emotional states that were not apt for cocaine use. For example, most respondents restricted use to when they were in the company of friends and stated that they did not use the drug when socialising with their parents and/or other family members. While a number admitted that there were times when they went 'overboard', cocaine use was generally confined to occasions when it was least likely to impact on work and other responsibilities. Respondents' also made reference to the importance of the individual's emotional and/or psychological state at the time of use.

If I had to work the following day I wouldn't take it. If I was hungry I wouldn't want to suppress my appetite for a while because I would want to have a meal. I would say that if I had a lot on my mind, if I was stressed or if there was an awful lot going on at work and in my life in general and I didn't want to deal with a hangover ... because at the end of the day if I go off and do some coke I am going to have a pretty bad alcohol hangover too because I tend to do the two together. And you think you're superman regarding alcohol intake so if my head doesn't feel right at the time then I wouldn't be taking it. Usually for me, if I had a lot going on in general I would avoid it for that reason. And then you are either in the mood or you're not, it's like anything, you know.

The quotes above illustrate the range of informal social controls that are practised when people consume drugs. Other respondents drew attention to how they regulate their intake of cocaine during the course of a night out.

I would take cocaine more during the early part of an evening and then just let it peter out. What I don't like is coming in at three o'clock in the morning and sitting there wide awake and not being able to sleep. So, for myself I would have the bulk at the beginning of the early part of the evening and then later in the evening have one or two lines just for a perk. And then when I get home, I am home to actually sleep.

While the level and range of 'control' measures practised by respondents varied across the sample, all mentioned conditions that were more or less apt for cocaine use. Overall, it would appear that respondents perceived the risks associated with cocaine use to be minimal, in terms of the drug's potential to cause physical and/or psychological harm. Interestingly, two respondents expressed concern about the legal risks associated with the possession and use of controlled substances.

> *The illegality of it is a huge worry because other than the fact that I use drugs for recreation, I am a 100 per cent law-abiding citizen. I pay my taxes etc. So, it is very hard to keep reminding yourself that you are actually a criminal. But you do, you actually have to remind yourself on occasion. Even though you are a really nice bloke, you are actually a criminal and if you get caught you could well end up inside ... and the repercussions could be huge from a legal, family, work point of view. Huge repercussions.*

The majority, however, felt that it was relatively easy to conceal their use of cocaine and that the chances of getting 'caught' were small or negligible.

> *I would never worry about being stopped because I can't really see what provocation there would be for the police to stop me.*

> *I know it's a class A drug but I usually wouldn't worry. I wouldn't want to get caught but I usually wouldn't worry much so long as I am not carrying too much.*

To summarise, cocaine was viewed as a relatively innocuous substance and users did not consider cocaine use to have negative repercussions on their health or well-being. None expressed concern about any short- or long-term health implications associated with their personal use of the drug and many felt that cocaine was 'safer' than other drugs.

3.6.11 Summary and Conclusion

Respondents in the current study described themselves as social/recreational drug users. Across the ten individuals interviewed, use was relatively modest and none of the respondents could be described as heavy users of cocaine. All respondents funded their cocaine and other drug use through legitimate income. Cocaine use was clearly integrated into social events; it was shared in social settings, sometimes in small intimate groups and, at other times, in the context of larger social gatherings. Cocaine was thought to facilitate communication and to induce feelings of self-confidence. The stimulating properties of cocaine, in conjunction with a 'controlled' high, were particularly attractive characteristics of the drug experience. This dynamic was important, particularly to more regular users, who did not wish cocaine to encroach on their normal activities and/or their physical and psychological well-being.

While the frequency of use varied across the group, most could be classified as 'monthly', 'weekend' or 'intermittent' cocaine users. Variation in frequency of use among recreational cocaine users has been documented previously by Green, Pickering, Fosster, Power & Stimson (1994) in their UK sample. Practically all respondents in this study reported the concurrent use of alcohol and other drugs during cocaine-using events. In fact, the vast majority had extensive drug repertoires. The combined use of licit and illicit drugs is far from atypical in the current European context. Nabben (2000), for example, found that among clubbers and ravers in Amsterdam, half used illicit drugs in combination with alcohol. A considerable number of the current study's respondents had gone through a phase of regular weekend use. While ecstasy was rated highly, all former regular users had reduced their intake of the drug owing to the significant negative repercussions following sustained use. For this group, cocaine was perceived to be 'lighter' and 'cleaner' and did not interfere with the user's desired level of functioning and well-being. Henderson (2000) similarly found that club-goers in Liverpool explained their cocaine use in terms of the drug being perceived as a 'healthy' alternative to ecstasy.

The majority of respondents expected to find themselves in social settings where cocaine was available and practically all intended to use cocaine at some time in the future. Reports indicated that the street price of cocaine varied between £50 and £80 per gram. However, conspicuous differences emerged in respondents' level of contact and association with local cocaine distribution networks. Those who socialised regularly in users' circuits had superior and more reliable access routes to cocaine.

Relatively few disadvantages associated with cocaine emerged from respondents' reports but most drew attention to the high cost of cocaine and to the poor quality of available supplies. Others commented on their observations of friends and acquaintances during sessions of use and felt that cocaine consumption sometimes produced undesirable, self-indulgent behaviour, including arrogance and greed. Few respondents reported that they themselves had experienced negative physical or psychological side-effects following cocaine use.

Social settings have been shown to influence a range of drug-taking behaviours (Becker, 1963; Young, 1971; Zinberg, 1984). Cohen (1989) claims that settings and individual responses largely determine not only the effects of use but also the choice of drug in particular contexts. Respondents in this study used a range of informal control mechanisms in an effort to regulate their cocaine intake and to minimise potential negative consequences of use. They also recognised settings not suited to cocaine use and avoided the drug in these contexts. Decorte (1999) has documented similar control strategies among a sample of cocaine and crack cocaine users in Belgium. In the current study, respondents prioritised work, friendships and their partners, and did not wish to jeopardise these relationships. Specifically, they did not allow cocaine or other drug use to impinge on their performance in the workplace. Reference was made to a range of circumstances under which the drug was not used, including during working hours and in the company of parents and/or other family members. Respondents also considered their own emotional and physical well-being prior to using cocaine.

None of the study's respondents reported 'problems' as a result of their cocaine use and none considered their current intake to be worrying or damaging, certainly in the short term. Claims that they, the users, and not the drug, maintained 'control', emerged strongly from their reports. This is interesting since the concept of 'loss of control' seems to be better adapted to current perspectives on illicit drug use (Cohen & Sas, 1992), with rather less attention to, and understanding of, controlled drug use. The majority of respondents considered the addictive potential of cocaine to be low, certainly from a personal viewpoint. Indeed, it is claimed that in many circumstances, cocaine is enticing rather than addictive (Hammersley & Ditton, 1994). Drug dependence is, of course, strongly mediated by the circumstances, disposition and views of the user (Zinberg, 1984). The cocaine users in this study did not fear addiction; neither did they believe that they were susceptible to developing a dependent relationship with cocaine, owing largely to a belief in their ability to control and regulate their intake of the drug.

3.7 Cocaine Use in Ireland: Discussion and Conclusion

The drug scene in Ireland has undergone dramatic change during the past decade and has become increasingly diverse according to age, drugs of choice, availability and price. National and local surveys of youthful populations indicate a clear upward trend in the range of drugs used, suggesting that recreational drug use has become a more obvious feature of adolescent lifestyles. At the other end of the drugs spectrum, long-term opiate users, many of whom are known to drug treatment services, appear to have extended their repertoire from heroin and methadone to poly-drug patterns. Benzodiazepines have been identified as a primary supplement to opiate users' drug intake (Farrell et al., 2000; Rooney et al., 1999). The propensity of cocaine, particularly in its injectable and smokeable forms, to appeal to this endemic group of heavy users is an issue of critical concern.

This research has attempted to build up a picture of cocaine use nationally, using available indicators of drug use/misuse and the perceptions of key informants and drugs workers. The research did not set out to estimate the prevalence of cocaine use; rather, it aimed to provide information on the nature of cocaine use, with specific reference to particular sub-groups, namely, recreational and problem drug users. In the absence of previous research on the topic, a multi-method approach, using several indicators, was judged to be the most effective means of analysing the current cocaine situation.

The findings strongly suggest increased availability and use of cocaine. Law enforcement statistics point to an upward trend in the availability of cocaine. In addition, the study has repeatedly noted the ease with which users can obtain cocaine. Although population and school surveys indicate that only small numbers use cocaine experimentally or intermittently, this current research provides evidence of individuals who use cocaine regularly for recreational purposes. Reference was made by most study respondents to the visibility of cocaine on the club and pub scenes, a development which was regarded as recent. While there is no systematic evidence of widespread cocaine use, the broad picture uncovered is one of increased likelihood of cocaine use among certain groups of recreational poly-drug users. The extent, nature and frequency of cocaine use among such groups, however, remain unclear.

Coupled with a possible expansion of cocaine use within the recreational drug scene, are signs of increased cocaine use among opiate users who come from more deprived urban areas, particularly within Dublin City. While cocaine has clearly been 'around' for some time, supply and availability appear to be stronger than previously. The reports of a diverse range of drugs workers and service providers confirm that this development is recent, certainly no more than three years old. Impressionistic accounts also strongly suggest that cocaine use has become a more conspicuous and accepted drug option.

It is important to state that the nature of cocaine use is likely to be diverse and that the role and function of cocaine within the drug repertoires of social/recreational cocaine users is likely to differ substantially from that of 'seasoned', heavy and problematic opiate drug users (Chitwood & Morningstar, 1985; Hammersley & Ditton, 1994). In addition, routes of administration are likely to vary between the two groups. Social users interviewed for the purpose of this research ingested cocaine intranasally or orally, and did not consider their drug consumption as damaging or problematic. None had been exposed to crack cocaine and did not consider using cocaine in this form. On the other hand, available statistical indicators, coupled with the reports of drugs workers, suggest that cocaine use has become more apparent among clients in treatment for heroin misuse. As stated earlier, there is currently little knowledge or understanding of preferred patterns of cocaine use, or of dominant routes of cocaine administration among problem drug users. This information is essential if cocaine's role in the drug repertoires of opiate users is to be fully understood. Furthermore, an understanding of smoking versus injecting cocaine rituals would greatly enhance knowledge and awareness of the possible range of health risks associated with cocaine use.

It would be premature to conclude, on the basis of the current study, that cocaine is a major 'drugs issue', or that the spread of cocaine use to neighbourhoods where heroin use is concentrated, is imminent or inevitable. Further research and monitoring of drug trends at local level is required to confirm or, alternatively, discount the proposition that cocaine is an expanding 'problem'. Despite this, heroin epidemics, both here and in the United Kingdom, have taught us that particular communities are susceptible to drug outbreaks (Dean, Bradshaw & Lavelle, 1983; O'Kelly, Bury, Cullen & Dean, 1988; O'Brien & Moran, 1997; Comiskey, 1998; Parker, Bakx & Newcombe, 1988; Pearson, 1989; Parker et al., 1998; Egginton & Parker, 2000). If cocaine continues to be easily available and gains acceptance among drug users, it may have the potential to find its way into communities that traditionally attract drug problems. In this sense, the current research might be appropriately viewed as an 'early warning sign' (Parker et al.,

1998) of cocaine's emergence, thus, signifying the opportunity to monitor the situation and 'get ahead'. In this context, a cautious response to possible signs of increased cocaine use is more appropriate than either outright rejection of the possibility, or hysteria and over-reaction.

3.8 References

Adler, P. (1990). Requirements for inductive analysis. In E. Y. Lambert (ed.), *The Collection and Interpretation of Data from Hidden Populations.* NIDA Research Monograph, 98.

Balding, J. (1998). *Young People and Illegal Drugs in 1998.* Health Education Authority: School Health Education Unit, University of Exeter.

Baker, O. & Marsden, J. (1994). *Drug Misuse in Great Britain.* London: Institute for the Study of Drug Dependence.

Barnard, M., Forsyth, A. & McKeganey, N. (1996). Levels of drug use among a sample of Scottish schoolchildren. *Drugs: Education, Prevention and Policy, 3,* (1), 81-89.

Becker, H.S. (1963). *Outsiders: Studies in the Sociology of Deviance.* New York: Free Press.

Bisset, F. (1997). *Ecstasy and Young People.* Dublin: National Youth Federation/Health Promotion Unit.

Biernacki, P. & Waldorf, D. (1981). Snowball sampling: Problems and techniques in chain referral sampling. *Sociological Methods and Research, 10,* 141-163.

Blanken, P. & Barendregt, C. (1997) 'Cocaine Smoking and Craving in a Natural Context: The relationship between setting, drug taking pattern, cocaine craving and subsequent drug taking behaviour'. Paper presented at the 8th International Conference on the Reduction of Drug Related Harm, 24-27 March 1997, Paris, France.

Boekhoutvan Solinge, T. (1998). Drug use and drug trafficking in Europe. *Tijdschrift voor Economische en Sociale Geografie, 1,* 100-105.

Bottomley, A. K. & Pease, K. (1986). *Crime and Punishment: Interpreting the Data.* Milton Keynes: Open University Press.

Bottomley, T., Carnwath, T., Jeacock, J., Wibberley, C. & Smith, M. (1997) Crack cocaine - tailoring services to user need. *Addiction Research, 5,* 3, 223-234.

Boyatzis, R. E. (1998). *Transforming Qualitative Data: Thematic analysis and code development.* CA: Thousand Oaks, Sage.

Brian, K., Parker, H. & Bottomley, T. (1998a). *Evolving Crack Cocaine Careers.* Research Findings No 85. London: Home Office Research and Statistics Directorate.

Brian, K., Parker, H. & Bottomley, T. (1998b). *Evolving Crack Cocaine Careers: New users, quitters and long term combination drug users in N.W. England.* Manchester: Department of Social Work and Social Policy, University of Manchester.

Brinkley, A., Fitzgerald, M. & Greene, S. (1999). *Substance Use in Early Adolescence: A study of rates and patterns of substance use among pupils in Dublin.* Dublin: Eastern Health Board and European Commission.

Byrne, R. (2000). 'Opioid-Related Deaths Investigated by the Dublin City and County Coroners in 1999: Background, analysis and prevention initiatives'. Unpublished. Dublin: Department of Social Studies, Trinity College.

Byrne, R. (2001). 'Opiate-Related Deaths Investigated by the Dublin City and County Coroners in 1998, 1999 and 2000'. Unpublished. Dublin: The Addiction Research Centre, Trinity College.

Chitwood, D. D. & Morningstar, P. C. (1985). Factors which differentiate cocaine users in treatment from nontreatment users. *International Journal of the Addictions, 20,* 449-459.

Choquet, M. & Ledoux, S. (1990). The use of official data in measuring patterns of drug use in the community: merits and limitations. In M. Plant, C. Goss, W.

Keup & E. Osterberg (eds) *Alcohol and Drugs: Research and policy.* Edinburgh: Edinburgh University Press and World Health Organisation. pp 95-109.

Cohen, P. (1989). *Cocaine Use in Amsterdam in Non Deviant Subcultures.* Amsterdam: Instituut voor Sociale Geografie.

Cohen, P. (1996). 'Notes on (Methods of) Drug Use Prevalence Estimation and Other Drug Use Research in a City.' Presentation for the Joint Seminar, 'Addiction Prevalence Estimation: Methods and Research Strategies', 10-14 June 1996, Strassbourg, France.

Cohen, P. & Sas, A. (1992). 'Loss of Control over Cocaine: Rule or exception?' Paper presented at the American Society of Criminology, New Orleans, 3-7 November 1992.

Comiskey, C. (1998). 'Estimating the Prevalence of Opiate Use in Dublin, Ireland during 1996'. Unpublished.

Commission on Narcotic Drugs (2000). *Drug Information Systems: Principles, structures and indicators.* Report from Commission on Narcotic Drugs: Forty-third session, Vienna, 6-15 March 2000.

Corkery, J. M. (2000). Snowed under. Is it the real thing? *Druglink*, May/June, 12-15.

Corrigan, D. (1997). *Facts about Drug Abuse in Ireland.* Dublin: Health Promotion Unit, Department of Health.

Dean, G., Bradshaw, J. & Lavelle, P. (1983) *Drug Misuse in Ireland, 1982-1983. Investigation in a north central Dublin area and in Galway, Sligo and Cork.* Dublin: The Medico Social Research Board.

Decorte, T. (1999). 'Informal Control Mechanisms Among Cocaine and Crack Users in Antwerp (Belgium: Summary of the main findings'. Paper presented at the Summer School for European Post-Graduate Students in Social Sciences, 2 August - 5 September 1999, Aarhus (Denmark).

Denehan, C., Clarke, M. & Liossis, C. (submitted). A survey of drug exposure and alcohol usage amongst university students: a preliminary report. *Journal of Psychological Medicine.*

Ditton, J., Hammersley, R., Philips, S., Forsyth, A., & Khan, F. (1996). *A Very Greedy Drug: Cocaine in context.* Amsterdam: Harwood Academic Publishers.

Douglas, J. D. (1976). *Investigative Social Research: Individual and team field research.* London: Sage Library of Social Research.

Egginton, R. & Parker, H. (2000). *Hidden Heroin Users: Young people's unchallenged journeys to problematic drug use.* Manchester: SPARC, Department of Social Policy and Social Work, University of Manchester.

EMCDDA (European Monitoring Centre for Drugs and Drug Addiction) (1999). *Annual Report on the State of the Drugs Problem in the European Union 1999.* Luxembourg: Office for Official Publications of the European Communities..

Erickson, P. G., Adlaf, E. M., Murray, G. F., & Smart, R. G. (1987). *The Steel Drug: Cocaine in perspective.* Lexington, Mass.: Lexington Books.

Farrell, M., Gerada, C. & Marsden, J. (2000). *External Review of Drug Services for the Eastern Health Board.* Dublin: Eastern Health Board.

Fischman, M. W. & Foltin, R. W. (1991). Cocaine and the amphetamines. In I. Belle Glass Routledge (ed.) *The International Handbook of Addiction Behaviour,* London: Routledge.

Friel, S., Nic Gabhainn, S. & Kelleher, C. (1999). *The National Health & Lifestyle Survey.* Galway: Health Promotion Unit, Department of Health and Children and Centre for Health Promotion Studies, National University of Ireland, Galway.

Frischer, M. & Taylor, A. (1999). Issues in assessing the nature and extent of local drug misuse. In C. Shark, B. A. Kidd & A. D. Sykes (eds) *Illegal Drug Use in the United Kingdom.* Aldershot: Ashgate.

An Garda Síochána (1991). *Report on Crime 1990.* Dublin: The Stationery Office.

An Garda Síochána (1992). *An Garda Síochána Annual Report 1992.* Dublin: The Stationery Office.

An Garda Síochána (1993). *An Garda Síochána Annual Report 1993.* Dublin: The Stationery Office.

An Garda Síochána (1994). *An Garda Síochána Annual Report 1994.* Dublin: The Stationery Office.

An Garda Síochána (1995). *An Garda Síochána Annual Report 1995.* Dublin: The Stationery Office.

An Garda Síochána (1996). *An Garda Síochána Annual Report 1996.* Dublin: The Stationery Office.

An Garda Síochána (1997). *An Garda Síochána Annual Report 1997.* Dublin: The Stationery Office.

An Garda Síochána (1998). *An Garda Síochána Annual Report 1998.* Dublin: The Stationery Office.

Garretsen, H. & Toet, J. (1992). The use of administrative data on health for estimating the prevalence of drug use. In H. F. L. Garretsen, L. A. M. van de Goor, Ch. D. Kaplan, D. J. Korf, I. P. Spruit & W. M. de Zwart (eds) *Illegal Drug Use: Research methods for hidden populations.* Proceedings, Invited Expert Meeting, 29 - 30 October 1992, Rotterdam.

Gleeson, M., Kelleher, K., Houghton, F., Feeney, A. & Dempsey, H. (1998). *Teenage Smoking, Drug and Alcohol Use in the Mid-West.* Limerick: Department of Public Health, Mid-Western Health Board.

Green, A., Pickering, H., Fosster, R., Power, R. & Stimson, G. (1994). Who uses cocaine? Social profiles of cocaine users. *Addiction Research, 2,* (2), 141-154.

Grube, J. W. & Morgan, M. (1986). *Smoking, Drinking and Other Drug Use Among Dublin Post-Primary School Pupils.* General Research Series, Paper No 132. Dublin: The Economic and Social Research Institute.

Grube, J. W. & Morgan, M. (1990). *The Development and Maintenance of Smoking, Drinking and Other Drug Use among Dublin Post-Primary Pupils.* General Research Series, Paper No 148. Dublin: The Economic and Social Research Institute.

Grund, J.-P. C., Adriaans, N. F. P. & Kaplan, C. D. (1991). Changing cocaine smoking rituals in the Dutch heroin addict population. *British Journal of Addiction, 86,* 439- 448.

Hammersley, R. & Ditton, J. (1994). Cocaine careers in a sample of Scottish Users. *Addiction Research, 2,* (1), 51-71.

Henderson, S. (2000). 'Protecting and Promoting the Health of Clubgoers in Liverpool: A social market report'. Report on expert meeting on qualitative drug research and emerging trends, EMCDDA, Lisbon, 4-5 December 2000.

Hay, G. (1998). Estimating the prevalence of substance misuse. In M. Bloor & F. Wood (eds) *Addictions and Problem Drug Use: Issues in behaviour, policy and practice.* London: Jessica Kingsley Publishers.

Hibell, B., Andersson, B., Bjarnason, T., Kokkevi, A., Morgan, M. & Narusk, A. (1997). *The 1995 ESPAD Report: Alcohol and other drug use among students in 26 European countries.* Stockholm and Strasbourg: The Swedish Council for Information on Alcohol and Other Drugs, Stockholm, and Council of Europe, Pompidou Group, Strasbourg.

Hibell, B., Andersson, B., Ahlstrom, S., Balakireva, O., Gjarnasson, T., Kokkevi, A. & Morgan, M. (2000). *The 1999 ESPAD Report: Alcohol and other drug use among students in 30 European countries.* Stockholm and Strasbourg: The Swedish Council for Information on Alcohol and Other Drugs, Stockholm, and Council of Europe, Pompidou Group, Strasbourg.

ISDD (1996). *Drug Abuse Briefing: a guide to the effects of drugs and to the social and legal facts about their non medical use Britain.* London: Institute for the Study of Drug Dependence.

Jackson, T. M. (1997). *Smoking, Alcohol and Drug Use in Cork and Kerry.* Cork: Southern Health Board.

Korf, D. J. (1992). Administrative data on criminal justice: the validity of drug seizures as indicators for trends in drug use. In H. F. L. Garretsen, L. A. M. van de Goor, Ch. D. Kaplan, D. J. Korf, I. P. Spruit & W. M. de Zwart (eds) *Illegal Drug Use: Research Methods for Hidden Populations.* Proceedings: Invited Expert Meeting, 29-30 October 1992, Rotterdam.

Lindensmith, A. (1947). *Opiate Addiction.* Bloomington, IN: Principia Press.

Loughran, H. (1999) Drug policy in Ireland in the 1990s. In S. Quin, P. Kennedy, A. O'Donnell & G. Kiely (eds) *Contemporary Irish Social Policy.* Dublin: University College Dublin Press.

McCracken, G. (1988). *The Long Interview.* Newbury Park, CA: Sage.

McElrath, K. & McEvoy, K. (2000). *Ecstasy Use in Northern Ireland.* Belfast: Department of Sociology and Social Policy and Institute of Criminology and Criminal Justice, Queens University of Belfast.

Marsden, J., Griffiths, P., Farrell, M., Gossop, M. & Strang, J. (1998). Cocaine in Britain: Prevalence, problems and treatment responses. *Journal of Drug Issues*, 28, 225-242.

Mayock, P. (2000), Choosers or Losers? *Influences on young people's choices about drugs in inner-city* Dublin. Dublin: The Children's Research Centre, Trinity College.

Murphy, T., O'Mahony, P. & O'Shea, M. (1998). *Ecstasy Use among Irish People: A comparative and interdisciplinary study.* Cork: The Centre for European Social Research and The Department of Law, National University of Ireland, Cork.

Murphy, S., Reinarman, C. & Waldorf, D. (1989). An 11-year follow-up of a network of cocaine users. *British Journal of Addiction, 84,* 427-436.

Nabben, T. (2000). 'Combined Use of Alcohol and Illicit Drugs'. Paper presented at the 11th Annual Conference of The European Society for Social Drug Research, 21-23 September 2000, Trinity College, Dublin.

NIDA (1999). *Cocaine Abuse and Addiction.* Research Report Series. Washington D.C.: National Institute on Drug Abuse.

O'Kelly, R., Bury, G., Cullen, B. & Dean, G. (1988) The rise and fall of heroin use in an inner city area of Dublin. Irish Medical Journal. 157, 2, 35-38.

O'Brien, M. & Moran, R. (1997). *Overview of Drug Issues in Ireland, 1997.* Dublin: Drugs Misuse Research Division, The Health Research Board.

O'Brien, M., Moran, R., Kelleher, T. & Cahill, P. (2000). *National Drug Treatment Reporting System, Statistical Bulletin, 1997 and 1998.* National Data and Data by Health Board Area. Dublin: The Health Research Board.

O'Neill, M. & O'Connor, A. M. (1999). *Drug Using Women Working in Prostitution.* Dublin: The Women's Health Project, Eastern Health Board.

Parker, H., Bakx, K. & Newcombe, R. (1988). *Living with Heroin: The impact of a drugs 'epidemic' on an English community.* Manchester: Open University Press.

Parker, H. & Bottomley, T. (1996). *Crack Cocaine and Drug-Crime Careers.* Manchester: Department of Social Policy and Social Work, University of Manchester.

Parker, H., Bury, C. & Egginton, R. (1998). *New Heroin Outbreaks amongst Young People in England and Wales.* London: Police Research Group: Crime Detection and Prevention Series, Paper 92.

Pearson, G. (1989). Heroin use in its social context. In D. T. Herbert & D. M. Smith (eds) *Social Problems and the City: New Perspectives.* New York: Oxford University Press.

Pinger, R. R., Payne, W. A., Hahn, D. B. & Hahn, E. J. (1995). *Drugs: Issues for today.* London: Mosby.

Power, R. (1989). Participant observation and its place in the study of illicit drug abuse. *British Journal of Addiction, 84,* 43-52.

Ramsay, M. & Partridge, S. (1999). *Drug Misuse Declared in 1998: Results from the British Crime Survey.* Home Office Research Study 197. London: Home Office.

Reinarman, C., Murphy, S. & Waldorf, D. (1994). Pharmacology is not destiny: the contingent character of cocaine abuse and addiction. *Addiction Research, 2,* (1), 21-36.

Rooney, S., Kelly, G., Bamford, L., Sloan, D. & O'Conor, J. J. (1999). Co-abuse of opiates and benzodiazepines. *Irish Journal of Medical Science, 168,* (1), 36-41.

South, N. (1995). Drug: Control, crime and criminological studies. In M. Maguire, R. Morgan & R. Reiner (eds) *Oxford Handbook of Criminology.* Oxford: Oxford University Press.

Stimson, G. V. (1987). The War on Heroin: British policy and the international trade in illicit drugs. In N. Dorn & N. South (eds) *A Land Fit for Heroin? Drug policies, prevention and practice.* London: Macmillan.

Stimson, G. V., Fitch, C., Rhodes, T. & Ball, A. (1999). Rapid assessment and response: methods for developing public health responses to drug problems. *Drug and Alcohol Review,* 18, 317-325.

Sutton, M. & Maynard, A. (1993) Are drug policies based on 'fake' statistics? *Addiction, 88,* 4, 455-458.

Waldorf, D., Murphy, S., Reinarman, C. & Joyce, B. (1977). *Doing Coke: An ethnography of cocaine users and sellers.* Washington D.C.: The Drug Abuse Council.

Waldorf, D., Reinarman, C. & Murphy, S. (1991). *Cocaine Changes: The experience of using and quitting.* Philadelphia: Temple University Press.

Wiebel, W. W. (1990). Identifying and gaining access to hidden populations. In E. Y. Lambert (ed.) *The Collection and Interpretation of Data from Hidden Populations.* NIDA Research Monograph 98. Washington D.C.: National Institute on Drug Abuse.

World Health Organisation (1992). *The ICD-10 Classification of Mental and Behavioural Disorders: Clinical descriptions and diagnostic guidelines.* Geneva: World Health Organisation.

Young, J. (1971). *The Drugtakers: The social meaning of drug use.* London: MacGibbon & Kee.

Zinberg, N. E. (1984). *Drug, Set and Setting: The basis for controlled intoxicant use.* New York: Yale University Press.

Znaniecki, F. (1934). *The Method of Sociology.* New York: Farrar and Rinehart.

Chapter 4

Women, Children and Drug Use[1]

Eimear Farrell

4.1 Introduction

This paper provides an overview of the issues relevant to women and children affected by drug misuse in Ireland. It attempts to bring together very disparate sources of information in order to gain an understanding of the main issues facing women drug users and their children. The main areas covered are:

4.2   Historical and Cultural Background
4.3   Epidemiology of Female Drug Use
4.4   HIV/AIDS, Women, Children and Drug Use
4.5   Drug Use among Female Prisoners
4.6   Pregnancy and Drug Use
4.7   Children and Drug Use
4.8   Demand Reduction (Prevention, Treatment and Care) and Female Drug Users
4.9   Barriers to Service Access
4.10   Conclusion
4.11   References

One of the most striking features of the available Irish research is the emphasis on pregnancy and drug use, and the scarcity of studies focusing on children of drug users.

---

[1] This chapter was written in 1999 as a 'Key Issues' chapter for inclusion in Moran, R., O'Brien, M., Farrell, E. & Dillon, L. (1999). National Report on Drug Issues Ireland 1999. Internal document. Dublin: Drug Misuse Research Division, The Health Research Board. Only National Drug Treatment Reporting System figures have been updated in the current chapter.

4.2 Historical and Cultural Background

According to the United Nations Drug Control programme (UNDCP), female involvement in drug use may be divided into three categories:

1. female non-drug users with drug-abusing families or partners;
2. females who consume drugs illicitly; and
3. females who are involved in the production and/or distribution of drugs.

In Ireland, very little is known about both non-drug-using women who have a drug-using partner or family, and women who are involved in the production and/or distribution of drugs.

No estimate is available of the number of women affected by familial drug use. However, a number of support groups have been set up for parents and partners of drug users. These support groups include the Coolmine Family Association and a group established for parents of drug users, entitled 'Le Chéile' (Together), which was established in 1993 but has since been discontinued.

The only Irish data available on women and drug production and distribution are police statistics on drug offences. These statistics indicate that between 1990 and 1994, approximately 14 per cent of people charged with drug offences were female (An Garda Síochána, 1991, 1992, 1993, 1994). In the following two years (1995 and 1996), this figure decreased, with about 10 per cent of drug-related offences being committed by women (An Garda Síochána, 1995, 1996). In 1997 this figure almost doubled, increasing to 22 per cent (An Garda Síochána, 1997). There is some anecdotal evidence that women in general, and pregnant women in particular, are increasingly being used in drug trafficking, which may explain the sudden increase in the percentage of women being charged with drug-related offences in 1997.

Although more information is available on women drug users in Ireland relative to the other two categories, it is not possible to examine long-term trends, as the collection of epidemiological data on drug use is a relatively recent phenomenon.

4.3 Epidemiology of Female Drug Use

An important issue when considering women and drug use is the extent to which male and female drug users differ in terms of drug-using history, patterns of risk behaviour and health issues.

The main source of information on gender differences and drug use in Ireland is the National Drug Treatment Reporting System (NDTRS), which provides statistics on treated drug misuse. An analysis of the NDTRS data for 1998 indicates that almost a third (30%) of drug users presenting for treatment were female. Male and female clients were similar in age, the mean age of female clients being 24 and the mean age of male clients being 25 (NDTRS)[2]. As with the general population, women seeking treatment were more likely to be classified as lone parents (9%) than were men (0.3%). Women were also more likely to be living with a drug-using partner: 36 per cent of women lived with a drug user compared to 22 per cent of men. This finding may relate to the fact that women are generally more likely to be introduced to drugs by a male partner (Ettore, 1992). The majority of both male (70%) and female drug users (75%) seeking treatment were unemployed. Interestingly, more women (88%) than men (78%) reported that opiates were their primary drug of misuse. However, a lower proportion of male (35%) than female (39%) users reported that they were currently injecting. In terms of risk behaviour, of those who were currently injecting, women (28%) were slightly more likely to be sharing injecting equipment than were men (25%).

Gender differences in drug usage, risk behaviour and health have also been studied among drug users attending an inner-city Dublin needle exchange programme (Cox, O'Shea & Geoghegan, submitted for publication). Over a year and a half, 934 consecutive new attendees at the needle exchange were interviewed. The study found that female clients were significantly younger than male clients and were more likely to inject their primary drug daily. Women were also more likely to suffer from injecting-related problems such as difficulty finding injecting sites. Men were less likely to have a partner who was injecting and less likely to be living with an injecting drug user. In terms of risk behaviour, women were more likely to share injecting equipment with their sexual partner and to report recent sharing of injecting paraphernalia. However, women had a shorter interval between injecting and attending a needle exchange than did men. In terms of health and general well being, women were more likely to

---

[2] National Drug Treatment Reporting System.

report weight loss and abscesses and were less likely to have had a hepatitis B vaccination than men. Women were also more likely to report mental health problems such as depression, suicidal tendencies, isolation and anxiety. However, women were more likely to have visited a general practitioner in the last three months and to have a medical card. Thus, the findings suggest that women were more likely than their male counterparts to engage in risk behaviour, but were more likely to acknowledge these difficulties and to seek help.

Summary

Consistent with the European situation, about a quarter of drug users who present for treatment in Ireland are female (EMCDDA, 1998). Although fewer women than men are captured in the treatment figures, research suggests that women in Ireland are more likely to suffer negative consequences from drug use than men. It also suggests that women in Ireland are more likely than men to engage in risk behaviour, to be living with a drug-using partner and to suffer from drug-related health problems.

4.4   HIV/AIDS, Women, Children and Drug Use [2]

Drug use can have serious health-related consequences, particularly in relation to HIV and hepatitis B and hepatitis C. While no national information is available on hepatitis B and C, statistics on the incidence of HIV in the population are routinely published by the Department of Health and Children. These statistics contain information on the percentage of HIV-positive cases that are related to intravenous drug use (IDU).

As Table 4.1 indicates, from January 1986 to December 1998, 42 per cent of all those who tested positive for HIV (n=1,986) were IDUs. Of these, almost a quarter (24%) were female. During the same period, a total of 149 children were deemed 'at risk' of becoming HIV positive, representing 7.5 per cent of all HIV-positive cases. The HIV statistics for children do not indicate the route of infection and, therefore, it is not known to what extent HIV among children is attributable to maternal drug use or other sources, e.g. transfusions or heterosexual or sexual transmission.

---

[2] See Chapter 2 for a discussion of the HIV/AIDS figures up to the end of 1999.

TABLE **4.1**

**Total Number of Known HIV Cases in Ireland: IDU Related, by Gender;
and Children at Risk. Numbers and Percentages.
Cumulative figures January 1986 - December 1998.**

Total HIV Cases	IDU Cases	Female IDUs	Male IDUs	Children at Risk
1,986	844 (42%)	202 (23.93%)	628*	149 (7.5%)

Source: Department of Health and Children.
* In 14 of the 844 IDU-related cases of HIV, the gender was not known.

The available statistics for AIDS present a similar picture. Two-fifths (41%) of the 650 AIDS cases diagnosed between January 1986 and 31 December 1998 were IDU related, of which, again, a quarter were female (see Table 4.2). An age breakdown is also available for AIDS cases, which indicates that twenty-six cases of AIDS (representing 4% of all AIDS cases) occurred among children under the age of 15. Unlike the HIV figures, the AIDS figures for children provide information on the route of infection. These figures indicate that from 1982 to 1998, thirteen children born to IDUs developed AIDS, representing 2 per cent of all AIDS cases over this time period.

TABLE **4.2**

**Total Number of AIDS Cases in Ireland: IDU-Related, by Gender;
among Children < 15; and among Children born to IDUs.
Numbers and Percentages. Cumulative Figures January 1986 - December 1998.**

Total AIDS Cases	IDU-Related AIDS Cases			AIDS Cases among Children Aged < 15	AIDS Cases among Children born to IDUs
	Total	Gender Breakdown			
		Male	Female		
650	266 (41%)	200 (75.2%)	66 (24.8%)	26 (4%)	13 (2%)

Source: Department of Health and Children.

Figures are also available for AIDS-related deaths (see Table 4.3). These figures indicate that between 1982 and 1998, 44.6 per cent of AIDS-related deaths were IDU related, and of these, 26.4 per cent were female. An age breakdown of known AIDS deaths shows that eleven (3.3%) occurred among children under the age of 15. The figures also reveal that eight children (representing 2.4% of all AIDS-related deaths) born to IDUs are reported to have died from AIDS.

TABLE 4.3

Total Number of AIDS Related Deaths in Ireland: IDU-Related, and Gender; among Children < 15; and among Children born to IDUs.
Numbers and Percentages. Cumulative Figures January 1986 - December 1998.

Total AIDS Deaths	IDU-Related AIDS Deaths			AIDS-Related Deaths among Children Aged < 15	AIDS-Related Deaths among Children born to IDUs
	Total	Gender Breakdown			
		Male	Female		
332	148 (44.6%)	109 (73.6%)	39 (26.4%)	11 (3.3%)	8 (2.4%)

Source: Department of Health and Children.

It is also possible to identify trends in known cases of IDU-related HIV among women and known cases of HIV among children (see Table 4.4). An analysis of these figures over a three-year period (1996-1998) indicates that the proportion of IDU-related cases of HIV among females more than doubled in 1998, compared with 1997 and 1996. Similarly, the number of new cases among children doubled between 1997 and 1998. This may be a reflection of increased testing for HIV among pregnant women. Routine antenatal testing for HIV was introduced in 1999, in order to allow a mother infected with HIV to receive special treatment that could reduce the likelihood of her baby becoming infected by up to 66 per cent (Department of Health and Children, 1999b). The testing was introduced following a five-year study (1992-1997), which estimated the incidence of HIV among new-borns, using unlinked, anonymous antenatal HIV screening. The screening was carried out on blood specimens routinely collected for rubella serology from pregnant women attending antenatal clinics. A total of 287,099 tests were carried out over the five years, of which 64 were positive for HIV, giving an incidence rate of 0.02 per cent. However, the extent to which HIV-positive results were drug related is unknown.

TABLE 4.4
Ireland 1996 - 1998. Number of IDU-Related HIV Cases among Women, and Number of New Childhood Cases. Numbers and Percentages.

1996		1997		1998	
Women	Children	Women	Children	Women	Children
3 (15%)*	8	3 (14%)*	10	10 (38.4%)*	20

Source: Department of Health and Children.
* Percentages are calculated based on the total number of new, IDU-related HIV cases.

A study of HIV infection among women attending thirteen genitourinary medicine/HIV clinics in England, and one clinic in both Dublin and Edinburgh, found that women in Dublin and Edinburgh were more likely to have contracted the disease through IDU rather than sexual intercourse (MRC Study Group, 1996). For over two-thirds of the seventy-three women interviewed in Dublin and for four-fifths of the forty-two women interviewed in Edinburgh, the most probable route of transmission was drug use; whereas in London (n=266) and in the rest of England (n=19), only one-fifth (21%) of women were thought to have been infected through drug use. Although not directly comparable, an analysis of Irish statistics on the route of infection among women with AIDS (collected by the Department of Health and Children) indicates that, across all cases, a smaller percentage of women contracted AIDS as a result of drug use than is suggested by the MRC study. The Department of Health and Children statistics indicate that 54 per cent of registered female AIDS cases were IDU related (Department of Health and Children, 1999a).

Although basic epidemiological data are available for the incidence of HIV, very little is known about the needs of female drug users with HIV. However, one Dublin study has investigated the needs of HIV-positive women by consulting with HIV-positive women and healthcare workers involved in their care (Butler & Woods, 1992). The results indicate that Dublin women who were HIV-positive were primarily concerned with taking care of their families and saw their own health problems as being of secondary importance. The healthcare workers interviewed stated that HIV-positive women in Dublin tended to be young, working-class and to have contracted HIV through IDU and/or sexual relationships with drug-using men. When asked about the services available to

HIV-positive women, respondents acknowledged that, while a broad range of services was available, many of these were poorly co-ordinated. They also felt that there was a lack of practical support for those who were ill and that the drug services could not yet be described as 'user friendly'. It was also suggested that HIV-positive women did not take up health and social services to the same extent as men for two reasons. Firstly, women were often too busy with child-minding and other chores to avail of services and, secondly, they feared being labelled as 'unfit' mothers. However, since this study was conducted, there has been a major expansion of drugs services.

Summary
The proportion of female IDU-related HIV and AIDS cases is similar to the ratio of male to female drug users in treatment. Approximately one-quarter of IDU-related AIDS and HIV cases occur among women. The number of IDU-related HIV cases appears to have increased in recent years. Very little information is available about the needs of female IDUs with HIV/AIDS. One study suggests that HIV-positive drug-using women with children may be inhibited from seeking treatment owing to concerns about being seen as an 'unfit mother' (Butler & Woods, 1992).

4.5 Drug Use among Female Prisoners

Drug use among women in prison has received some attention in Ireland. A study of 100 consecutive women prisoners entering the main prison in Dublin suggests that drug misuse is a significant problem among the female prison population. The study, conducted over a six-week period in February and March 1994, found that sixty of the women interviewed had used drugs (Carmody & McEvoy, 1996). Among the sixty women who used drugs, heroin was the most frequently-used drug (95%), followed by methadone (83%) and benzodiazepines (83%). Cocaine had been used by almost two-thirds (63%) of the women, and amphetamines by over a third (35%). All except one of the sixty women were using drugs on imprisonment, as indicated by a positive urine test for opiates. The vast majority of the drug-using women (92%) were daily users, and 86 per cent stated that injecting was the primary route of administration. Almost half of those who had injected had shared a needle in the last month. Interestingly, 43 per cent of the women described methadone as one of their drugs of first choice.

When asked about their history of drug treatment, four-fifths of the drug-using women stated they had been detoxified at least once, and over half (57.1%) had been detoxified three or more times. Over half (53%) had been detoxified in prison. About half the drug-using women had been on methadone maintenance at some stage in the past, and 43.3 per cent were on methadone maintenance at the time of imprisonment. The results of the study also indicate a possible link between drug use and psychiatric problems among this population, as 61 per cent of the forty-nine women who had received psychiatric treatment were drug users.

A more recent survey of male (n=1,148) and female prisoners (n=57) found that women prisoners were more likely than their male counterparts to smoke heroin and/or inject drugs (Allwright, Barry, Bradley, Long & Thornton, 1999). Almost three-fifths (59.6%) of the women surveyed, reported smoking heroin, compared to 45.2 per cent of male respondents. Three-fifths (59.6%) of women also reported ever injecting, compared to just over two-fifths (42.4%) of men.

Summary
The results of two surveys of the prison population suggest that opiate use is a serious problem among women in the Irish prison system. Furthermore, women in prison appear more likely than their male counterparts to smoke or inject heroin (Allwright et al., 1999).

4.6 Pregnancy and Drug Use

Maternal drug addiction was first recognised as a problem in Ireland in 1981, when nine babies were born to heroin-addicted mothers attending one of the main maternity hospitals in Dublin (Ryan, Arthurs, Kelly & Fielding, 1982). This represented a marked increase, as the previous eight years (1973-1980) had seen only a total of six babies born to heroin-addicted mothers. A socio-demographic profile of thirteen of the fifteen opiate-addicted mothers indicated that the majority (69%) were under 20 years of age, half were unemployed and only one had completed post-primary education. All the women were heavy cigarette smokers. One third of the women had a parent with a nervous or psychiatric history and less than a quarter described their relationship with their parents as good. Furthermore, nine of the thirteen women had received treatment for emotional or psychiatric disorders. In terms of physical health, seven had hepatitis and two had venereal diseases. The profile of the partners of these women indicates that twelve of the thirteen partners were drug addicts and only two gave the mother any support or assistance when she was pregnant. Although none of the infants were small for gestational age, anxiety about the social conditions of mothers led to longer hospitalisation and separation of the infants from their mothers. This study also investigated the short-term outcome for the infants and their mothers. The results indicated that two mothers were drug free, two had developed serious neurotic illnesses following withdrawal, one was hospitalised for a drug-related psychiatric illness, and the remainder were still addicted. Furthermore, three of the babies had been taken into care.

A similar profile of the pregnant drug user emerges from a study of the characteristics of thirty pregnant women who attended the National Drug Advisory and Treatment Centre, Jervis Street, Dublin, between 1969 and 1983 (Kelly, Roche, Stafford-Johnson & Honeyman, 1983). Interestingly, the age of first contact for pregnant drug users was, on average, a year and a half younger than non-pregnant women attending the same service. The study found that the majority (87%) of pregnant opiate users had left school before the age of 16. A third of the women were married and living with their husbands. The majority (83%) of the women's partners misused drugs or alcohol and over a third (37%) had a record of crime or violence. Only three of the women had partners who gave them consistent support and assistance during their pregnancies. Almost three-quarters (73.3%) of the women had a behavioural disorder or received psychiatric treatment prior to drug taking. An investigation of the family background of these women revealed that a quarter of the women had mothers who had a psychiatric problem or were excessive drinkers. A third of the women's fathers were excessive drinkers and a quarter were reported as being violent or criminal. On a more positive note, over half the women received on-going support from their mothers, and almost half were described as having a good relationship with their own family. Similar to the earlier study, babies born to drug-addicted mothers were hospitalised for longer and therefore separated from their mothers at an early age. The women appeared reluctant to avail of healthcare services both prenatally and postnatally. Only half the women attended for antenatal care at an early stage. Many of the mothers were resistant to any health board involvement postnatally and many refused to attend for the normal developmental checks and vaccinations.

In terms of outcome, at least 65 per cent of the mothers were known to have returned to serious drug misuse (21.5% lost contact with the Centre and their outcome is unknown), and three (11%) remained drug free. In the majority of cases (70.3%), babies were in the care of their mother; in the remainder of cases, babies were either in the care of a grandmother or jointly cared for by the grandmother and the mother (11%), or had been adopted (11%). In two cases, the outcome was unknown.

Another retrospective study, of twenty-nine narcotic-addicted mothers and their forty-two babies born between 1982 and 1985, found that the average maternal age was 23 and, in all cases where information was available (29 of 38 pregnancies), all fathers were drug users (Thornton, Clune, Maguire, Griffin & O'Connor, 1990). Twenty-three of the twenty-nine mothers (79%) were on a methadone maintenance programme during pregnancy, but they all continued to use heroin intermittently. All the women were from socially-deprived areas and all, except one, smoked cigarettes. In terms of physical health, four of the mothers had a hepatitis B infection and thirteen had a previous history of hepatitis B infection. In comparison to a matched control group, babies born to heroin-using mothers had significantly lower birth weights and mean gestational periods and were more likely to develop jaundice. In addition, heroin-using mothers made fewer antenatal visits and were admitted to hospital more often and for longer stays than were the control group. A high incidence of withdrawal symptoms was recorded, with 84 per cent of babies suffering some symptoms of withdrawal. The incidence of multiple births (i.e. twins) was also much higher among drug-using mothers (10.5%) compared to the control group (1.2%).

Another similar study, conducted in 1988, examined the characteristics and treatment progress of forty-five opiate addicts referred to a treatment centre between 1984 and 1986 (O'Connor, Stafford-Johnson & Kelly, 1988). The psycho-social profile of this group indicates that all were unemployed, were regular smokers and had left school on average at the age of 14. The average age of first use of heroin was 16.5 years and the average age at the time of the study was 23.3 years. Almost half (46.6%) of the women had used heroin intravenously as their first illicit drug. The average length of time on drugs before referral was three years. Interestingly, the majority of mothers (86.7%) were attending the clinic for an average of 2.5 years before becoming pregnant. Four-fifths were single. Almost all (95.5%) had been convicted of a criminal offence. In terms of family profiles, nearly half the women had fathers who suffered from alcoholism and a third had mothers who suffered from alcoholism or depression. Over half (55.5%) reported severe family disharmony. This study also investigated HIV status and found that fifteen of the forty-five women were HIV positive. Over half the women had a history of hepatitis B infection. Almost half (45%) the women responded positively to treatment during pregnancy, as indicated by regular attendance, non-abuse of drugs (as detected through the results of supervised urinalysis), discontinuation of criminal behaviour and improved awareness of their children's needs (O'Connor et al., 1988).

A six-year follow-up of these women was conducted, focusing on their drug use and the outcome for their children (Keenan, Dorman & O'Connor, 1993). On follow-up, seven of the forty-five women (15%) could not be contacted. Of the remaining thirty-eight, ten were on methadone maintenance, eighteen were either attending another service or abusing chaotically, three had become drug free and seven had died from drug-related illnesses. Of the women who had died, four had died from AIDS and three from drug overdoses, two of which were accidental and one deliberate. Over the six-year period, all but two of the women (4.5%) had re-attended at the treatment centre at least once, and twenty-five women (55.6%) had attended at least four times. There was an increase in the number of women with HIV, from one-third of the group to over half the group (53.4%) during the six years (1986-1992), and a quarter of the fifteen children born to HIV-positive mothers before 1996 had become HIV positive. More worrying was the fact that fourteen of the eighteen HIV-positive women, who were still alive, were not attending any medical service on a regular basis. This may be, in part at least, related to a fear of being seen as an unfit mother, a reason cited earlier among HIV-positive women for not accessing services (Butler & Woods, 1992). The increase in the incidence of HIV among the women is interpreted by the authors as signifying instability and poor compliance with advice and treatment. On a more positive note, since 1986 only three of the women (6.6%) had contracted hepatitis B infections, compared to twenty women (45%) prior to 1986. Over half the women (55.5%) had no further children and there was also a decrease in the level of criminal activity among the women. Before 1986, nearly all the women (97.8%) had a forensic history. However, since 1986 just over half the women had been in contact with the criminal justice system.

All the studies discussed so far have specifically focused on opiate-using mothers. A more recent study has examined the prevalence of drug and alcohol use in an obstetric population in the Dublin area (Bosio et al., 1997). This prospective study involved anonymous urinalysis of 504 'first-visit' antenatal patients and 515 postnatal patients six weeks after delivery. The study found that the prevalence rate for drug use in antenatal patients was 2.8 per cent; the corresponding postnatal figure was 5.6 per cent. Cannabis was found to be the most commonly-misused substance. Women who tested positive for drugs antenatally were almost twice as likely to be single, unemployed and on a second or subsequent pregnancy. The higher postnatal rate of drug use is interpreted as possibly indicating a more responsible pattern of behaviour during pregnancy, in an effort to minimise exposure of the foetus to chemical substances. Bosio et al. (1997) conclude that drug abuse does not appear to be a serious problem among Dublin's pregnant population. However, they acknowledge that drug users may present late in pregnancy, as has been found in previous studies of pregnant opiate users (Kelly et al., 1983; Thornton et al., 1990).

Summary
The research available on opiate addiction and pregnancy in Ireland suggests that opiate-dependent pregnant women are a high-risk medical category, with many psychological and social problems. Numerous studies have shown that opiate-using pregnant women tend to be young, poorly educated, regular tobacco smokers, and from socially-deprived areas. Research also indicates that these women tend to be involved with a partner who also misuses drugs and to have poor family relationships, or come from families with a history of alcohol misuse, drug abuse and/or psychological problems. The level of psychological difficulties among the families of these women is consistent with findings internationally that dysfunctional family life, rather than poverty, seems to be one of the most significant predisposing factors to drug use (United Nations Drug Control Programme, 1997).

4.7 Children and Drug Use

In Ireland, the issue of how children are affected by parental drug dependence is emerging as a new social and clinical concern (Hogan, 1998). In an exploratory study, Hogan had noted that little is known about the social and psychological effects on children of parental drug use: 'the main focus of existing research in Ireland has been on prenatal chemical exposure of children to drugs rather than on postnatal social exposure' (Hogan, 1997: 4).

Although the prevalence of parenthood among drug users is unknown, the fact that the majority of treated drug abusers in Ireland are of child-bearing years (Moran et al., 1997), coupled with anecdotal evidence that many drug users are parents, suggests that a large number of children may be affected by drug abuse. The statistics for treated drug misuse indicate that, in 1998, 9 per cent of women presenting for treatment stated, when asked about their living status, that they were lone parents (NDTRS)[3]. However, the NDTRS does not capture parental status per se and the number of drug-using women who have children is likely to be much higher. A study of the parental status of clients attending a voluntary drug agency (Ana Liffey Project) found that over three-quarters of the 186 women attending the service during 1992 were parents (Woods, 1994). Over three-fifths (62.8%) of the 142 mothers were caring for their own children. A possible explanation for the high level of attendance of mothers at the voluntary agency may be that voluntary services are perceived as less threatening than statutory services among drug-using women with children (Woods, 1994). It is likely that some women with children may be reluctant to approach treatment services because of concerns about being seen as an 'unfit mother' (Butler & Woods, 1992).

One of the earliest references to children and drug misuse, in the Irish context, is a case study of a boy who had begun misusing drugs before his eleventh birthday (Ryan et al., 1982). The boy, who was 12 years old on admission to the Drug Advisory and Treatment Centre, had been abusing a number of drugs including diconal, palfium, cocaine and heroin for eighteen months. At this time, it was discovered the boy had chronic hepatitis B infection with cirrhosis. The boy was from a large family (he was third eldest in a family of ten), his father was unemployed and his mother suffered from a neurotic disorder with agoraphobic symptoms. He was also on probation, having broken into a car. He had been attending a special school for two years and had presented with behavioural problems at 7 years of age. Ryan et al. (1982) comment on the difficulties encountered in the hospitalisation and placement of very young offenders with drug problems, as exemplified by this case.

Another study, which is relevant in this context, although it does not focus on children *per se*, is a study that looked at the risks associated with methadone storage. Following a coroner's hearing into the death of a 3-year-old boy, who died after ingesting methadone stored in a baby's feeding bottle, a study was conducted to investigate the extent to which babies' bottles were used to measure

---

[3] National Drug Treatment Reporting System

and store methadone (Harkin, Quinn & Bradley, 1999). The study involved nine general practitioners, who asked 186 patients in receipt of a methadone prescription whether or not they used a baby's bottle to measure methadone, and if they had children under the age of 14. The results indicated that almost a quarter of patients (n=48) had used a baby's bottle to measure methadone in the previous month, and twenty-one (43%) of these had a child under the age of 14. Furthermore, seven patients had used a baby's bottle to store methadone in the previous month, and four of these had a child under the age of 14. Although it is difficult to draw conclusions from these findings, they suggest that the use of a baby's bottle to measure and/or store methadone may present a threat to the health of children

In an attempt to redress the lack of research on children of drug users in Ireland, Hogan (1997) is conducting a two-stage study on the social and psychological effects on young children of parental heroin use. The first part of the study, which involved a qualitative study of ten families, in which one or both parents were opiate users, has been completed. Interviews were conducted with thirty informants consisting of parents, teachers, professional workers and non-parental caregivers. The study found that all the children (n=10) in the sample had at least one parent who had been incarcerated and that the majority had experienced separation from their parents owing to parental drug use (Hogan, 1997). From the interviews with teachers and parents, it emerged that only a few children showed evidence of social-emotional problems; however, the majority were experiencing difficulties at school. Parents expressed three main concerns about how their drug use might impact adversely on their parenting. The first concern related to their pre-occupation with obtaining drugs, which might result in inadequate attention being paid to their children. The second worry was that their drug use would affect their social interaction with their children. The third related to a prevailing atmosphere of secrecy in the home owing to parental drug use and the possible development of distrustful relationships between the parents and children. Key workers interviewed were particularly concerned about the questionable quality and consistency of care-giving by drug-using parents, the danger of physical neglect, and the possibility that children might witness drug use. Interestingly, all these concerns were raised in a recent editorial in the journal *Addiction* (Barnard, 1999). Key workers also emphasised that there were a number of parents about whom no concerns existed and whose competence they stressed. Thus, as Barnard (1999) points out, it cannot be assumed that drug dependence automatically results in diminished capacity to parent adequately or that the development of children is necessarily adversely affected by parental drug use.

Hogan (1997) also identifies a number of variables that mediate the effects on children of parental drug use, including the living arrangements of the child, the social support available to parents, the extent to which one or both parents are in treatment, whether or not the drug-using parent is in treatment, the history of drug use and treatment, the age of the child when parents begin using heroin and whether or not this drug use is chaotic. Stage 2 of Hogan's study, which is currently under way, investigates the extent to which children are exposed to the drug culture and aims to examine the consistency and adequacy of care provided to children of drug users.

Summary

Although the extent to which children in Ireland are affected by drug misuse is unknown, a study of drug-using women attending a voluntary agency suggests that many drug-using women are also parents (Woods, 1994). Very little is known about the needs of children of drug users in Ireland; however, a study is under way that aims to investigate the needs of drug users and their children (Hogan, 1997). The first phase of this study has been completed and has found that the majority of children experienced separation from one or both of their parents owing to drug use. Parents, key workers and teachers interviewed expressed concerns about the possible impact of drug use on children. The study also identifies a number of variables such as the social support available to children and drug-using parents that can influence the extent to which parental drug use affects children.

4.8 Demand Reduction (Prevention, Treatment and Care) and Female Drug Users

A small number of initiatives have been developed specifically for women in Ireland. The focus of these initiatives has been on treatment, rehabilitation and care rather than prevention. There is at least one harm-reduction programme in place especially for women.

Harm Reduction

A harm-reduction programme for women sex workers who are using drugs has been set up by the Merchant's Quay Project, a voluntary organisation providing services to drug users and persons with HIV/AIDS in Dublin's city centre (Merchant's Quay Project, 1998). The harm-reduction programme is overseen by a healthcare worker and operates on a weekly basis, offering services such as needle exchange and condom distribution. The programme has produced some positive outcomes, with some clients subsequently progressing to the Mobile Clinic (a low-threshold service) and to detoxification programmes.

Treatment

Some treatment facilities in Ireland have support groups or drop-in times designated for women only (e.g. Ana Liffey Project). One service, the Merchant's Quay Project, accommodates mothers wishing to access the needle exchange, by allocating hours in the morning, found to be more suitable for women with children. However, there are very few treatment services dedicated to providing programmes specifically for women drug users. The treatment services available in Ireland specifically for women drug users include a drug-free residential programme, and services developed for pregnant women.

The Coolmine Therapeutic Community provides a residential drug-free programme specifically for women at Ashleigh House, Clonee, County Meath. This programme, based on the Minnesota Model,[4] involves an abstinence-orientated approach. At the time of writing there were twenty-five women participating in this programme. Ashleigh House is currently being renovated to accommodate mothers and their children, as part of a project funded through a Local Drug Task Force. When completed, the facility will allow five to ten mothers, with up to two children each, to participate in the programme.

A special programme for pregnant opiate addicts in Ireland was established by the then National Drug Advisory and Treatment Centre in 1984, in response to the growing numbers of pregnant clients attending the clinic (O'Connor et al., 1988). The programme involved low-dose methadone maintenance, weekly group therapy and fortnightly attendance at antenatal clinics (Keenan et al., 1993). Participants in the programme were also encouraged to attend

---

[4] Associated with the Alcoholics/Narcotics Anonymous programmes, the Minnesota model offers a 12 step programme to long term abstinence based on the idea that addiction is a disease. Devised by the Hazelden Hospital in Minnesota, the programme offers spiritual as well as practical guidance. (www.drugscope.org.uk)

programmes outside the clinic where appropriate. Postnatally, women were given advice about contraception and encouraged to address their addiction. Participation in the programme was conditional on non-consumption of drugs, as monitored by daily, supervised urinalysis, engagement in weekly group meetings, and attendance at antenatal care.

According to Williams & Kinsella (1990), other services available to pregnant opiate addicts in Ireland include group therapy, occupational therapy, individual counselling and support groups for family members. In Ireland, methadone maintenance is generally the preferred treatment option for pregnant opiate users for a number of reasons. Firstly, it is hoped that the prescription of methadone will reduce/eliminate illicit opiate misuse during pregnancy. Secondly, the administration of regulated methadone doses helps to reduce the risk of an infant developing withdrawal symptoms in the immediate postnatal period (Keenan et al., 1993). Thirdly, methadone maintenance encourages better antenatal care and a more stable drug environment for mother and child (Kelly et al., 1983).

The Eastern Health Board (EHB) employs three drug liaison midwives to make contact with substance-misusing pregnant women and to liaise between the obstetric hospitals and the drug-treatment services. The midwives are responsible for ensuring that the medical, psychological, obstetrical and social needs of each woman have been accurately assessed and for drawing up a detailed clinical/psychological/social care plan for each woman (Eastern Health Board, 1998).

A unit, which will provide intensive medical care to stabilise expectant drug-addicted mothers and improve neonatal outcome, is currently being planned and will be located in Dublin's Cherry Orchard Hospital (Vize, 1999). The twelve-bed facility will offer intensive medical treatment by a psychiatrist with a team of specially-trained nurses, and access to counselling and screening. Additionally, the unit will incorporate a facility for female addicts who have delivered and since destabilised, which will allow mother and baby to remain together while treatment is being administered. At present, only three of seventeen beds in the detoxification unit of the hospital are allocated to pregnant women requiring stabilisation. According to Dr Keenan, consultant psychiatrist in the EHB, the new unit should have a significant impact on the prevalence of neonatal complications and morbidity associated with opiate dependent pregnancies (Vize, 1999).

Care and Rehabilitation

At the time of writing, the most recent service plan for the largest health board area in Ireland (Eastern Health Board) has placed an increased emphasis on after-care and rehabilitation. Although there is no particular emphasis on women-only services, SAOL has been established, providing rehabilitation and support for women who are stable opiate users. SAOL stands for Seasamhacht, Abaltacht, Obair, Leann, meaning stability, ability, work and learning - the word 'saol' means life. The project, which began in 1995 in Dublin's north inner city, offers a two-year programme for sixteen women. The project aims to help clients move from addiction and dependency to self-direction and self-reliance. The programme incorporates a wide variety of activities, including literacy skills, English, creative writing, aromatherapy, relaxation and massage. It is based on the principles of social justice, equality and inclusion. A review of the programme by Weaver (1998) indicates that participants view the programme as a 'job', which gives them a perceived status in the community. Participants reported increased levels of self-esteem, ability to re-establish relationships with family members and becoming reintegrated into their communities as a result of the programme.

Summary

Very few services have been developed specifically for women. Some treatment centres accommodate women and children by having more flexible opening hours for this client group. There is one residential drug-free programme for women only. Services have also been developed for pregnant opiate users and a harm-reduction programme is in place in the Dublin area. A women-only rehabilitation service has also been established.

4.9 Barriers to Service Access

In examining the services available to female drug users and their children, it is also important to examine possible barriers, which would prevent or inhibit women from accessing services.

A recent Dublin study found that lack of childcare facilities is a barrier to accessing drug treatment, in particular for women (Moran, 1999). The research found that only nine of forty-five drug-treatment centres in Dublin provided crèche facilities. Interviews were conducted with a wide variety of personnel (including crèche leaders and workers, treatment staff, parents/guardians, and children attending the crèche) in six of the nine centres offering crèche facilities. The results indicate that crèches are perceived as playing an important role in the children's emotional, psychological and educational development. It was also found that crèche leaders facilitate mothers in their parenting by providing advice and help in relation to parenting skills. Furthermore, having access to a crèche influences parents' willingness to attend treatment and their psychological approach to treatment.

Butler & Woods (1992) found that HIV-positive female drug users were less likely to seek treatment, owing, in part at least, to fears of being judged an unfit parent and having their children taken into care by the State. Similarly, Hogan (1997), in her study of the psychological and social needs of the children of drug users, found that mothers' fears of having their children taken into care were quite pronounced.

Dunne (1994), in a study exploring the service needs of fifty female drug addicts, found that the vast majority (82.5%) had family support, mainly from their mothers. Consistent with other studies, the majority (71%) had drug-using partners. More worrying was the finding that half the women had partners who were described as violent. When asked what services were important to them, 'women-only support groups' were most frequently mentioned, followed by welfare, one-to-one counselling, crèche facilities, relaxation and parenting skills. The study concludes by recommending that female support groups with professional facilitation be established in each treatment centre and that crèche facilities be extended and improved in drug-treatment facilities.

Summary
Lack of crèche facilities and fears of being seen as an 'unfit mother' appear to be the main barriers facing Irish drug-using women seeking treatment. An analysis of the needs of drug-using women also suggests that female support groups are considered an important aspect of treatment.

4.10 Conclusion

It is apparent that research on women, children and drugs in Ireland has focused almost exclusively on pregnant opiate addicts. Consequently, there is a lack of information on how drug use affects women in general and how parental drug use impacts on children.

The available research suggests that Irish female drug users engage in more risk behaviour than their male counterparts, which has significant health implications, increasing their likelihood of contracting HIV and hepatitis B and C infections. The profile of the pregnant opiate user clearly indicates that these women are in need of a very high level of support. The high rate of drug use among women prisoners is also an issue of concern.

Lack of crèche facilities and fears of being seen as an 'unfit mother' appear to be two of the main barriers preventing women from accessing treatment. Consequently, an increase in the provision of crèche facilities would help more women gain access to services. Similarly, it appears that assurances need to be given to female drug users seeking treatment, that accessing services will not jeopardise their custody of their children.

The available indicators all suggest that female drug users have particular needs that require to be taken into account in service planning and provision. Much more research effort is needed into the issues surrounding drug use by women in Ireland and internationally.

4.11 References

Allwright, S., Barry, J., Bradley, F., Long, J. & Thornton, L. (1999). *Hepatitis B, Hepatitis C and HIV in Irish Prisoners: Prevalence and risk.* Dublin: The Stationery Office.

Ana Liffey Drug Project (1994). *Annual Report 1993.* Dublin: Ana Liffey Project.

Barnard, M. (1999). Forbidden questions: drug-dependent parents and the welfare of their children. *Addiction, 94* (8), 1109-1111.

Bosio, P., Keenan, E., Gleeson, R., Dorman, A., Clarke, T., Darling, M. & O'Connor, J. (1997). The prevalence of chemical substance and alcohol abuse in an obstetric population in Dublin. *Irish Medical Journal, 90* (4), 1-4.

Butler, S., & Woods, M. (1992). Drugs, HIV and Ireland: Responses to women in Dublin. In Dorn, N., Henderson, S. & South, N. (eds) *AIDS: Women, drugs and social care.* London: Falmer Press.

Carmody, P. & McEvoy, M. (1996). *A Study of Irish Female Prisoners.* Dublin: Stationery Office.

Cox, G., O'Shea, M. & Geoghegan, T. (submitted for publication). Gender differences in characteristics of drug users presenting to a Dublin syringe exchange. *Irish Journal of Psychological Medicine.*

Department of Health and Children (1999a). 'Anonymous Unlinked Antenatal HIV Screening in Ireland: Results for the period 4th Quarter 1992 to 4th Quarter 1997'. Internal Report. Dublin: Department of Health and Children.

Department of Health and Children (1999b). 'Press Release: Minister Cowen announces commencement of routine antenatal testing for HIV'. Dublin.

Dunne, C. (1994). 'Female Drug Users and Service Provision. A Study of Female Drug Users' Characteristics and Their Implications for Service Response'. MSc dissertation, University of Dublin.

Eastern Health Board (1998). *AIDS/Drug Addiction Services: Inventory of policies.* Dublin: Eastern Health Board.

EMCDDA (1998). *Annual Report on the State of the Drugs Problem in the European Union 1998*. Luxembourg: Office for Official Publications of the European Communities.

Ettore, E. (1992). *Women and Substance Abuse*. London: Macmillan Press.

An Garda Síochána (1991). *Report on Crime 1990*. Dublin: The Stationery Office.

An Garda Síochána (1992). *An Garda Síochána Annual Report 1992*. Dublin: The Stationery Office.

An Garda Síochána (1993). *An Garda Síochána Annual Report 1993*. Dublin: The Stationery Office.

An Garda Síochána (1994). *An Garda Síochána Annual Report 1994*. Dublin: The Stationery Office.

An Garda Síochána (1995). *An Garda Síochána Annual Report 1995*. Dublin: The Stationery Office.

An Garda Síochána (1996). *An Garda Síochána Annual Report 1996*. Dublin: The Stationery Office.

An Garda Síochána (1997). *An Garda Síochána Annual Report 1997*. Dublin: The Stationery Office.

Harkin, K., Quinn, C. & Bradley, F. (1999). Storing methadone in babies' bottles puts young children at risk. *British Medical Journal, 318,* 329.

Hogan, D. M. (1997). *The Social and Psychological Needs of Children of Drug Users: Report on exploratory study*. Dublin: The Children's Research Centre, Trinity College.

Hogan, D. M. (1998). Annotation: The psychological development and welfare of children of opiate and cocaine users: Review and research needs. *Journal of Child Psychology and Psychiatry, 39* (5), 609-620.

Keenan, E, Dorman, A. & O'Connor, J. (1993). Six year follow up forty five pregnant opiate addicts. *Irish Medical Journal, 162,* 252-255.

Kelly, M. G., Roche, D., Stafford-Johnson, S. & Honeyman, A. (1983). Drug addiction in pregnancy - The Irish scene. In Dennerstin, L. & Senechens, M. (eds) The young woman. Psychosomatic aspects of obstetrics and gynaecology. *Excerpta med, 618,* 119-129.

Merchant's Quay Project (1998). *The Merchant's Quay Project: Annual Report, 1997.* Dublin: The Merchant's Quay Project Drugs/HIV Service.

Moran, R. (1999). *The Availability, Use and Evaluation of the Provision of Crèche Facilities in Association with Drug Treatment.* Dublin: The Health Research Board.

Moran, R., O'Brien, M. & Duff, P. (1997). *Treated Drug Misuse in Ireland: National report, 1996.* Dublin: Health Research Board.

Moran, R., O'Brien, M., Farrell, E. & Dillon, L. (1999). National Report on Drug Issues, Ireland 1999. Internal document. Dublin: Drug Misuse Research Division, The Health Research Board.

MRC Study Group (1996). Ethnic differences in women with HIV infection in Britain and Ireland: The study group for the MRC collaborative study of HIV infection in women. AIDS, 10, 89-93.

O'Brien, M. & Moran, R. (1997). *Overview of Drug Issues in Ireland: A resource document.* Dublin: Drug Misuse Research Division, The Health Research Board.

O'Connor, J. J., Stafford-Johnson, S. & Kelly, M. G. (1988). A review of the characteristics and treatment progress of 45 pregnant opiate addicts attending the Irish National Drug Advisory and Treatment Centre over a two-year period. *Irish Journal of Medical Science, 157* (5), 146-149.

Ryan, W. J., Arthurs, Y., Kelly, M. G. & Fielding, J. F. (1982). Heroin abuse with hepatitis B virus-associated chronic active hepatitis in a twelve-year old child. *Irish Medical Journal, 75* (5),166.

Thornton, L., Clune, M., Maguire, R., Griffin, E. & O'Connor, J. (1990). Narcotic addiction: The expectant mother and her baby. *Irish Medical Journal, 83,* 139-142.

United Nations Drug Control Programme (1997). *World Drug Report.* Oxford: Oxford University Press.

Vize, E. (1999). First unit for pregnant addicts. *Medicine Weekly, 3* (25), 1.

Weaver, G. (1998). Educating Rita: Adult education and women's stories. ISDD *Drug Link, July/August,* 20-23.

Williams, H. & Kinsella, A. (1990). Depressive symptoms in opiate addicts on methadone maintenance. *Irish Journal of Psychological Medicine, 7,* 45-46.

Woods, M. (1994). Drug using parents and their children: The experience of a voluntary/non-statutory project. *Irish Social Worker, 12* (2), 10.

Notes On Authors
and
The Drug Misuse Research Division

Rosalyn Moran, MA, MSc, HDE

Rosalyn Moran is a research psychologist. She has conducted and managed social research in national, European and international contexts from public and private sector environments. She worked on the development of the Framework Programme for European Research and Development as an expert to the European Commission. She has published broadly in health and related areas. Currently, she heads up the Mental Health Research Division at the Health Research Board.

E-mail address: rmoran@hrb.ie

Lucy Dillon, BA

Lucy Dillon is a sociologist. She has carried out research in the areas of crisis pregnancy, methadone maintenance treatment and drug use in prison. She has expertise in the area of drug-related infectious diseases and drug use in the context of the criminal justice system.

E-mail address: lucy@hrb.ie

Mary O'Brien BA, Dip. Stats., Dip. Soc. & Soc. Res.

Mary O'Brien is a senior social researcher. She is responsible for the co-ordination of the National Drug Treatment Reporting System. She is the DMRD representative on national and European fora in relation to epidemiology of drug misuse, drug treatment demand, and drug related deaths. She is a member of a national committee on Joint Action against new synthetic drugs. Current research includes analysis of trends in drug misuse in Ireland and population survey work. She authors annual reports on treated drug misuse in Ireland.

E-mail address: mary@hrb.ie

Paula Mayock, BEd, MEd

Paula Mayock is a researcher at the Addiction Research Centre, Trinity College, Dublin. She has carried out research on drug use by young people and is continuing work in this area. She has also conducted an exploratory study on cocaine use in Ireland and will be undertaking further work on this topic as part of a European-wide study.

E-mail address: pmayock@tcd.ie

Eimear Farrell , BA, MSc

Eimear Farrell is a research psychologist. She has previously been involved in research in the field of education in Ireland and research into pathological gambling. She carried out research on perceptions of drug-related services while in the DMRD. In September 2000 she began her training on a full-time basis in the doctorate of clinical psychology programme in University College Dublin.

Brigid Pike, MA, MPhil, DBS

Brigid Pike is a writer and editor. She has worked on a range of policy, planning and research documents in the government and community sectors.

E-mail address: brigid.pike@oceanfree.net

Drug Misuse Research Division of the Health Research Board

The Drug Misuse Research Division (DMRD) is a division of the Health Research Board (HRB), a statutory body based in Dublin, and is involved in national and international research and information activities in relation to drugs and their misuse. The DMRD is funded by national and EU sources and contract research. International collaborators include the EMCDDA and Council of Europe Pompidou Group.

The DMRD maintains and develops the national epidemiological database on treated drug misuse in Ireland - the National Drug Treatment Recording System (NDTRS). The NDTRS provides comprehensive data on the numbers and characteristics of those treated for drug misuse in Ireland.

Current and recently completed research studies include research into trends in drug misuse; knowledge, attitudes and beliefs regarding drugs and drug users; drug service provision; crèche availability and use in drug treatment contexts; drug use, impaired driving and traffic accidents; drug use by prisoners and drug use in rural areas.

The DMRD is involved in information and dissemination activities at national and European levels. It publishes research studies on an ongoing basis. These publications are made available to all public and relevant specialist libraries in Ireland. The DMRD also publishes Drugnet Ireland twice yearly.

A new National Documentation Centre is being established in the DMRD as an initiative of the National Advisory Committee on Drugs (NACD).

More information on the work of the DMRD can be found on the Health Research Board's website at www.hrb.ie. A number of DMRD publications are available online. The website includes links to local and international sites providing drug-related information.

Health Research Board Publications since 1997

Dillon, L. (2001). *Drug Use among Prisoners: An exploratory study*. Dublin: The Health Research Board.

Moran, R., O'Brien, M., Dillon. L. & Farrell, E., with Mayock,P. (2001). *Overview of Drug Issues in Ireland 2000: A resource document*. Dublin: The Health Research Board.

O'Brien, A., Moran, R, & O'Brien, M. (2001). *Annotated Bibliography of Drug Misuse in Ireland*. Dublin: The Health Research Board.

Browne, C., Daly, A. & Walsh, D. (2000). *Activities of Irish Psychiatric Services 1998*. Dublin: The Health Research Board.

Bryan, A., Moran, R., Farrell, E. & O'Brien, M. (2000). *Drug-Related Knowledge, Attitudes and Beliefs in Ireland: Report of a nation-wide survey*. Dublin: The Health Research Board.

Daly, A. & Walsh, D. (2000) *Activities of Irish Psychiatric Services 1999*. Dublin: The Health Research Board.

Drug Misuse Research Division (2000) Drugnet Ireland (2). Dublin: The Health Research Board.

Drug Misuse Research Division (2000) Drugnet Ireland (3). Dublin: The Health Research Board.

Health Research Board (2000) *Making Knowledge Work for Health: Towards a strategy for research and innovation for health*. Dublin: The Health Research Board.

Mulvany, F. (2000) *Annual Report of the National Intellectual Disability Database Committee 1998/1999*. Dublin: The Health Research Board.

O'Brien, M., Moran, R., Kelleher, T. & Cahill, P. (2000) *National Drug Treatment Reporting System. Statistical Bulletin. 1997 and 1998*. National Data and Data by Health Board Area. Dublin: The Health Research Board.

Browne, C., Daly, A. & Walsh, D. (1999). *Activities of Irish Psychiatric Services 1997*. Dublin: The Health Research Board.

Health Research Board (1999) *Annual Report and Accounts, 1998*. Dublin: The Health Research Board.

Keogh, F., Roche, A. & Walsh, D. (1999) *"We Have No Beds…."*: An enquiry into the availability and use of acute psychiatric beds in the Eastern Health Board region. Dublin: The Health Research Board.

Moran, R. (1999) *The Availability, Use and Evaluation of the Provision of Crèche Facilities in Association with Drug Treatment*. Dublin: Drug Misuse Research Division, The Health Research Board.

Health Research Board (1998) *Annual Report and Accounts, 1997*. Dublin: The Health Research Board.

O'Brien, M. & Moran, R. (1998). *Overview of Drug Issues in Ireland: A resource document* . Dublin: The Health Research Board.

Keogh, F. & Walsh, D. (1997) *Activities of Irish Psychiatric Services 1996*. Dublin: The Health Research Board.

Moran, R., O'Brien, M., & Duff, P. (1997) *Treated Drug Misuse in Ireland: National report 1996*. Dublin: The Health Research Board.

National Intellectual Disability Database Committee. (1997) *Annual Report 1996*. Dublin: Health Research Board.

O'Higgins, K. & Duff, P. (1997) *Treated Drug Misuse in Ireland: First national report*. Dublin: The Health Research Board.